YEARN TO BURN

A Pyrography Master Class

Simon Easton

FOX CHAPEL
PUBLISHING

To Hazel
With lots of love, Mum.

No excuses now ... let your artistic talent flow --- and burn baby burn!
First Order -- "FAIRY GARDEN" please
love mum xx

Yearn to Burn: A Pyrography Master Class is an original work, first published in 2019 by Fox Chapel Publishing Company, Inc. The patterns contained herein are copyrighted by the author. Readers may make copies of these patterns for personal use. The patterns themselves, however, are not to be duplicated for resale or distribution under any circumstances. Any such copying is a violation of copyright law.

Finished project glamour photography by Mike Mihalo. Avebury (page 159) and owl (pages 105 and 162) photos are courtesy of Angela Norman. The "Eric" logo doodle on the Children's Reward Bank with Tokens project (pages 121–129) and the pattern (page 165) is courtesy of The Idol Dead.

ISBN 978-1-56523-986-9

Library of Congress Cataloging-in-Publication Data

Names: Easton, Simon, author.
Title: Yearn to burn : a pyrography master class / Simon Easton.
Description: Mount Joy : Fox Chapel Publishing, [2019] | Includes index. |
 Identifiers: LCCN 2019000161 (print) | LCCN 2019003548 (ebook) | ISBN
 9781607656432 (ebook) | ISBN 9781565239869
Subjects: LCSH: Pyrography.
Classification: LCC TT199.8 (ebook) | LCC TT199.8 .E285 2019 (print) | DDC
 745.51/4--dc23
LC record available at https://lccn.loc.gov/2019000161

To learn more about the other great books from Fox Chapel Publishing, or to find a retailer near you, call toll-free 800-457-9112 or visit us at *www.FoxChapelPublishing.com*.

We are always looking for talented authors. To submit an idea, please send a brief inquiry to acquisitions@foxchapelpublishing.com.

Printed in Singapore
First printing

Dedication

This book is dedicated with my sincere appreciation to the following people:

To my gorgeous wife, Jane, for her ongoing love and support.

To my beautiful daughter, Bethan, and my stepsons, Howell, Harry, and Freddie.

I will not be allowed to forget the pets . . . so thanks also to our Jack Russell, Pickle, and the gerbils, Luna and Fleur.

To the true friends out there who stand by me through thick and thin (some of whom also stand by me at the barrier of various rock concerts), and a special mention must go out to the following people: Rhys Miles, Jez Long, Tam Gale, Tim Emery, Jason Murphy, Barry Walker, Sarah Preston, Steve Pengilly, Sara Sayers, Will Smith, Nigel and Angela Norman, Chailey and Hayley Illman, Jon Chandler, Kim Pringle, Wayne Harvey, Gavin Johnson, Krishan Singh, Steve Dudden, Jason Soper, Adrian Hextall, John Elsdon, and Kay Dickinson.

From a crafting and creative perspective, a huge thank you to Bud Sperry, Katie Ocasio, and the crew behind the scenes at Fox Chapel Publishing; Pete Moncrieff-Jury at Bodrighy Wood; Lindsey White at Splatt Art; Colin Ellis at Dalescraft; Steve Jardine at Craftshapes; David Mounstephen and the team at Yandles & Sons Ltd; Ian Lockhart at Antex; Tony Kwasniak at GMC Publications; Terry Smart at Chestnut Products; Andrea Cooke at Picture It, Thatcham; Milan Bharadia of Kitty's Kombucha; Tim and Rachel Buxton, for the work space; plus Roger Mortimer and all of the guys at Sound Knowledge, Marlborough.

And I could not have tackled this book without the inspiration provided to me by numerous musicians and bands that display a truly independent spirit to keep fighting for the principles of creativity in the face of soulless industry adversity . . . so a massive shout-out to Ginger Wildheart, James, Frank Turner and the Sleeping Souls, Eureka Machines, Ryan Hamilton and the Harlequin Ghosts, The Idol Dead (especially to Polly and KC for allowing me to use your Eric logo!), CJ Wildheart, Massive Wagons, The Urban Voodoo Machine, Therapy?, Scott Sorry, Role Models, The Main Grains, The Scaramanga Six, Boss Caine, Chris Catalyst, The Slow Readers Club, Paul Miro, William the Conqueror, Terrorvision, Tax The Heat, Baby Chaos, The Dowling Poole, Tony Wright, Case Hardin, The Levellers, Exit_International, The Twilight Sad, The Spangles, Ferocious Dog, She Makes War, PowderKeg, and finally ("Never Outdrunk, Never Outsung") . . . The Wildhearts. Look them all up and have a listen; you won't regret it.

Massive kudos and respect also to Alastair Hercalees Duncan, who keeps many of the above bands going while they perform onstage. Cheers for the set lists, Dunc!

About the Author

Simon Easton studied a BA (Hons) Three-Dimensional Design degree at Manchester Metropolitan University, where he focused on woodturning, silversmithing, and pewterware. His pewter napkin ring set was one of the MMU winners of the Pewter Live 1999 competition and was displayed at Pewterers' Hall in London. He won a Precious Metals Bursary and a Grant from the Worshipful Company of Goldsmiths to produce design concepts that he had developed. The common theme in Simon's work at university was a decorative and textural feel, often rich in embellishment or pattern.

Before graduating in 2000, Simon's design for a decorative turned wooden bowl was selected for inclusion in the *onetree* project. This project, which toured the UK as an exhibition, stemmed from the use of one single ailing oak tree distributed to a range of artists, designers, manufacturers, and craftspeople. Every single part of the tree (from the leaves to roots) was used to create a stirring and diverse display of talent, which was also featured in a book published to accompany the tour. For the *onetree* exhibition, Simon created a decorative turned wooden bowl with a spun pewter insert, entitled "Wish, Hope, Dream, Everything."

Simon's crafting focus and love of wood led him to the art of pyrography, which he uses with a contemporary twist to create richly decorative items and gifts. The result is a diverse and exciting body of work released since 2007 under his business name of Wood Tattoos. He has created a varied range of works and commissions, regularly selling at craft fairs and galleries and accepting custom orders at *www.WoodTattoos.com*. He has also actively sought to help up-and-coming newcomers to the craft through demonstration events and online forums.

Simon is the author of *Woodburning with Style* (2010) and *Learn to Burn* (2013). The former is a comprehensive guide to the art of pyrography from start to finish, while the latter is a book of projects designed to help beginners build their confidence and abilities. Both books have received positive feedback from readers around the world. In February 2018, Simon also appeared live on UK television to spread awareness of pyrography as a craft, demonstrating during a feature and interview on Channel 4's *Sunday Brunch*.

You can keep up to date with his latest designs through his regular social media updates at *www.facebook.com/woodtattoos* or *www.instagram.com/wood_tattoos*.

Foreword

As I write this introductory section to my third book on the craft of pyrography, I'm approaching the tenth anniversary of my "Wood Tattoos" business. What started as a creative hobby intended solely to help me relax and kick back from the pressures of my day job obtained a momentum of its own right: before I knew it, I was creating a website, booking tables at craft fairs, taking commissions online, and registering myself as a crafts business. I'd only been burning "professionally" for around a year when Fox Chapel Publishing made contact out of the blue, asking me to write a book on my "style" of pyrography and contributing immensely to where I stand today.

I still get the same thrill out of starting work on a new commission for a customer. The excitement of developing a design to satisfy the needs of that individual, to make real the intangible idea in their head of a piece that they are envisaging, is an honor and a pleasure. I always try to involve the client in my creative processes by showing them the ideas as they progress, as this helps to reinforce the belief that the design would not be complete without them. They're not buying an anonymous mass-produced item from a generic store, they are a crucial part of creating something unique, something individual, something that will be cherished by the recipient for years to come. The item we create together is an original piece of inspired consequences, a project that has only come into fruition because of the personality, ideas, preferences, and history of both craftsperson and consumer.

My aim in this book, *Yearn to Burn: A Pyrography Master Class*, is to demonstrate ways to approach several projects through the use of woodburning, with my ideas and approaches only intended as a starting point for you, the avid reader and budding pyrographer. You can follow the guidance contained within these pages rigidly and recreate the designs that I've made, as these will help you to hone your pyrography skills and confidence if the craft is still new to you. As you become more comfortable and proficient, you can tinker with the suggested projects, adding your own take on them or adapting them into a style of your own choice. Ultimately, once you get to the point where your head is brimming with visions of your own invention, you can take elements from my work that you find useful or helpful as a starting point to enable you to develop your own design vocabulary.

I want you to appreciate that you are potentially in the same position as I was only a mere ten years ago. You've been bitten by the woodburning bug and are exploring what other makers have done before you, so that you can take your first tentative steps into the crafting world. You'll learn the techniques, experiment with ideas, and develop your own style through personal trial and error. Before you know it, people will be looking at what you can make and declaring that they trust you to make something special and meaningful for them, whether they are a family member, a friend, or a potential paying customer. Enjoy and treasure those moments, as they are a measure of your own abilities demonstrated through the faith that these people place in you to create something magical from just a quantity of raw materials, your trusted pyrography machine, and a sprinkling of imagination.

Keep on burning!

Contents

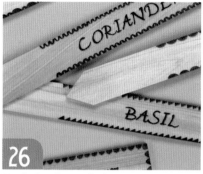

26
Herb Garden Label Set

41
Mandala-esque Table Set

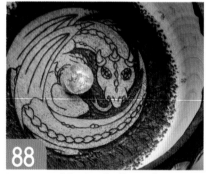

47
Celtic Knotwork Bangle

52
Art Nouveau Wall Organizer

81
Zodiac Solitaire Game Board

88
Dragon Table Catchall Bowl

95
Castle Kitchen Container

130
Christmas Eve Platter for Santa

141
Reversi Game Board and Counters

30 Engagement Ring Box

35 Texture Print Key Fobs

61 Dream Catcher Clock

67 Stained Glass Wall Sconce

74 Mirrored 3D Layer Picture Frame

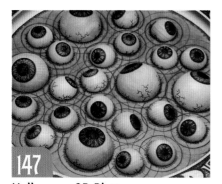

104 Owl Keepsake Box

112 Set List Text Art Frame

121 Children's Reward Bank with Tokens

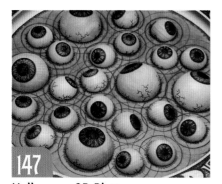

147 Halloween 3D Platter

Chapter 3: Patterns 154

Chapter 1: Tools, Hints, and Tips

Pyrography as a Craft

You would probably struggle to find a craft with a more dramatic name than pyrography, which literally translates to "writing with fire." No matter what surface you choose to work on creatively, the same principle and process applies, namely the application of heat to a surface to make a range of decorative marks. Irrespective of the origin of the name, this is not a craft for fireworks, explosions, and drama. Pyrography is a hobby that requires patience, skill, and a steady hand in order to master the techniques and become confidently proficient in your own ability.

Pyrography Machines

The most important decision you will make when starting out in pyrography is which machine to purchase. Pyrography equipment falls into two general categories: "solid point" or "hot wire" machines. In terms of price and flexibility, solid point machines are often regarded as entry-level kits, as they are cheaper and slightly less versatile than hot wire machines. Many budding crafters start with a less expensive kit in order to see if pyrography is the right craft for them, before moving onto a more advanced machine at a higher price once "bitten by the woodburning bug." Pyrography machines are durable, reliable, and well built, as they are relatively simple tools, so they also hold their value well, which means you can often find secondhand kits for sale.

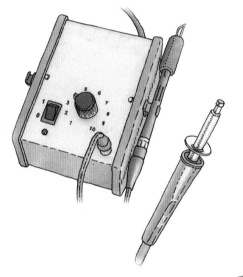

Solid Point Machines

The solid point machine resembles a traditional soldering iron in terms of physical appearance, with the name deriving from the solid brass nibs that it uses. These kits are usually chunky in terms of their physical structure, as the heating element is contained within the pen handle itself; this can make them a little trickier to hold or work with, particularly when trying to create finely detailed drawings or over longer periods of use. The nibs are available in a range of shapes and sizes to create different marks and often feature shaped nibs that can be used as decorative stamps. These machines generally have no more than two heat setting options at the most, with many only having a simple "on/off" switch and no further adjustability.

Hot Wire Machines

Hot wire machines are named after the finer metal nibs that they utilize. As these pen tips are formed from finely shaped wire forms, they can be used for detailed work much more readily than a solid point machine. Hot wire machines typically consist of a base unit with a power switch and an adjustable temperature setting so that the heat of the pen can be increased or decreased to suit the user's needs. They have a separate pen that is attached by an electrical cord. Since the heating element is held within the base unit rather than the pen itself, the pens are usually smaller in size and, therefore, easier to hold and maneuver during use. Some manufacturers make "fixed" pens with a specific nib permanently fitted to its own handle, but most machines are also supplied with a pen with a range of different wire nibs that can be swapped as needed. These pens have a pair of holding posts at the tip with a screw mechanism or similar to secure the wire nibs in place and complete the circuit necessary to allow the heat to pass through.

The Pyrography Pen

As well as the type of pyrography machine that you elect to buy, it is also vital to consider your choice in terms of handling. Each unit (and most importantly the pen itself) has its own size, shape, and weight that must be kept in mind before you make a purchase. If you are going to be working on a design for a sustained period, the pen must be easy for you to hold in a comfortable yet relaxed grip. A pen that is too heavy or too awkward for you to hold will not be easy or enjoyable to work with, resulting in poor finished results and, ultimately, a lack of pleasure in what you are doing. If you can do so, visit a crafts supplier where you can handle a range of different machines first before spending your hard-earned money; you will not regret it in the long run!

I strongly believe that holding a pyrography pen should be as comfortable as holding a regular pen or pencil. You should be able to hold the pen in a natural, relaxed grip without any effort or strain. Most pyrography pens are designed to protect the user from any excess heat through insulated grip sections or guards to keep stray fingertips away from the business end; you must, therefore, bear this in mind when using the pen. Ultimately the pyrography pen needs more care and consideration than normal writing implements when it is being used due to the added risk of the generated heat.

General Safety Tips

Always take care with the nib of a pyrography pen. Metal can retain a residual heat for a long period of time even after the machine has been switched off. It is often easy to tell when nibs are hot while in operation, but you must be mindful to allow enough time for them to cool after use before you handle them again. If in doubt, use a pair of pliers to move them or test the nib against a piece of paper to see if it is still hot enough to make a burn mark on the surface. This is particularly important if you are planning on changing nibs regularly during a crafting session.

Make sure that your pen is secure when you place it down between uses. Some pyrography kits have a hook or holder on the side of the machine for this purpose; you can also get free-standing pen holders for some brands that allow you to rest it safely in place between sessions. For maximum safety, it is always best to turn the machine off when not in use, since it is easy for a pen to be accidently touched or to catch the cord on something.

Ventilation is also an important consideration when working, particularly when doing so for longer periods of time. Smoke and fumes can be harmful if inhaled, so consider using a mask and goggles

if you feel this is necessary; this may be especially beneficial if you are doing large areas of sustained heavy shading or similar. There are specialty extractor fan units available in the market that are targeted specifically for use by pyrographers. Alternatively, a small desk fan or something similar can assist in achieving the same result. Point the fan away from your work so that the smoke is drawn away from you as you burn. If the fan is used facing your working area, the breeze will cool the nib and may make it harder or slower for you as you try to create your design.

Keep your workspace tidy and free of clutter to reduce the chance of any accidents or problems. A protective heat-resistant mat is essential for protecting your table or desk; pieces of scrap wood, hardboard, or thick cardboard can be used as a low-cost alternative solution. Dispose of litter or waste from your workspace promptly, and ensure that you do not store any hazardous chemicals or substances near the area where your pyrography machine will be in use.

Take care to maintain your pyrography equipment during and between each use. Ensure that you take regular breaks when working for longer periods of time so that your hands do not become tired or painful through excessive effort. Do not work with a tangled cord, as this can lead to accidents if your movement becomes impeded. Do not use your machine if you believe it to be faulty or damaged in any way; get the kit checked by a qualified technician or the manufacturer if necessary.

Nib Choice

Nibs for pyrography machines are available in a range of sizes and shapes in order to allow you to make different lines and marks on your surface of choice. The principle is the same whether your machine is a solid point or hot wire; each shaped nib lends itself to a specific quality of line, pattern, or texture. Most pyrography machines have the capacity for the nibs to be changed in some way, whether this is through swapping a new nib into the holding posts of the pen unit or by using a range of different pens that all have a different nib fixed to them.

The range of shaped nibs available is vast, but you will need to consider the limitations of your chosen machine. Some pens will only fit nibs that are specifically made by the same manufacturing company, so make sure you do not make a wasted purchase by buying incompatible accessories. This principle applies to most solid point machines because of the to the methods of fitting the metal nibs into the pen, which is usually through a screw thread technique or some similar method.

Basic shaped wire nibs are not generally subject to such restrictions and can be used between a range of pyrography machine brands due to the generic structure of a pen with holding posts. This makes them a very affordable option, as you can shop around for the supplier or manufacturer offering the best prices and value for money without being tied to one company's products. Wire nibs are often available in packs containing an assortment of different sizes or shapes, so you can also search for the brand that supplies the option most suited to your own individual preference.

When speaking to people interested in taking up pyrography as a hobby, I am regularly asked about nibs and which ones I would recommend as being essential to own. I always explain that pyrography is like many other arts or crafts—such as painting or woodturning, for example—in that there are an almost infinite range of brushes or tools available, but you do not need to own every single one in order to achieve the best results. In my view and from my own experience, I always state that there are four main types of pyrography nib that I would describe as essential for any crafter. I believe that you can create a wide range of marks and effects with just those four nib types alone. My basic pyrography nib palette would include the following four types of nibs described below and on page 14.

- A writing nib creates a broad range of lines and marks smoothly over various surfaces. This can include a basic single wire loop nib (shaped in a "U") or a more specialty option such as a ballpoint nib.

- A fine or bladed nib is used to burn crisp, sharp lines or for work that requires fine detail. The nib can be drawn easily over the surface for linear marks, or the sharp point can be used to create precise features of a design. This type includes the skew- or spear-point nib.

- A spoon point nib was named for its distinctive spoon-shaped profile. This nib is possibly one of the most versatile forms available and is one of my personal favorites (as described on page 15).

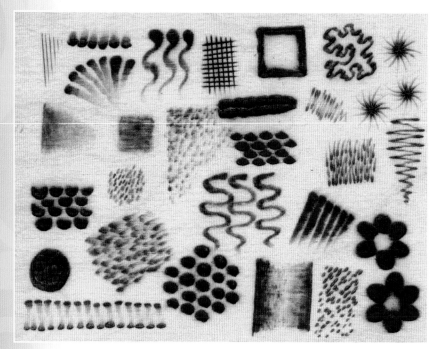

- A broad shading nib is used to fill in larger areas of tone more efficiently due to the increased size of the surface area that is in contact with the material to be burned. These nibs are available in a range of different shapes and forms.

If you were restricted to working with just a single pyrography nib, my recommendation would always be to choose the spoon point nib due to its adaptability over a wide range of effects. The lip of the nib can be used to create fine lines and sharper marks. The nib itself can be rotated so that the bowl of the spoon point is brought in contact with the surface, creating a softer and broader mark that is suited to shading or similar effects. With just this single nib, I could happily work on and complete a wide range of pyrography designs and would not feel restricted or limited in any way through only having a single "weapon" in my arsenal. The spoon point is my nib of choice for versatility and flexibility.

With hot wire machines, you also have the option to buy a quantity of Nichrome™ pyrography wire that you can then cut to length and use to make your own wire nibs. These can be shaped into any form that you like in order to make them just right for a mark that you need to incorporate in your chosen project. You can coil the wire to increase the surface area for a broader shading effect, or you can consider filing or shaping the wire loop into a finer point or edge for more detailed linear work; the options are endless.

Creating Marks

The marks that you create with your pyrography machines are affected by a range of factors. These include the temperature setting that you have chosen, the shape or type of nib, the pressure that you use to apply the nib to the surface, and the duration of time that you leave the nib in contact. Adjusting any one of these variables will enable you to change the sort of mark, line, or shade that you create. Higher temperatures, increased pressure, or longer contact will result in darker or more distinct marks, while the opposite approach will create lighter and more delicate effects.

Take care to practice your mark-making techniques on scrap wood before you move onto a final piece. I always recommend that new crafters build up a library or scrapbook of mark-making results so that you can learn what you can achieve with different nibs and techniques. You can then retain these for future reference. This will help you have something to look back through when you are trying to achieve a certain line, texture, or pattern in a project. It will also help you to learn how to use your pyrography machine to the best of your ability without ruining

a potential finished piece. The use of heat to create marks on a surface can be quite unforgiving, so it is always best to practice your techniques as much as possible before translating them into something you are creating for a purpose.

Use your pyrography pen in the same way that you would use a regular pen or pencil to draw with. Make sure that your grip is comfortable yet relaxed and try to work in the direction that your hand and wrist naturally want to move; attempting to go against that in a forced manner can result in lines that are uneven or of a poor quality. It is common to move the piece of material that you are working on numerous times as you burn a design, so that it is positioned in a way that you can make the marks naturally and without any unnecessary strain or discomfort.

Shading Techniques

Shading helps to create a sensation of form, depth, and texture in your pyrography designs. As with basic mark making, it is another technique that requires practice to become adept and confident. Broader shading nibs are extremely useful for creating areas of tone without looking scratchy or uneven. I recommend starting any shading at the lighter end of the tonal spectrum; if you shade too darkly at the beginning of a design, it can be very hard to amend the error. Starting with lighter tones and gradually building up to the darker shades through careful application or "layers" reduces the prospect of ending up with something that you cannot correct. Start with a lower temperature and don't press too hard on the surface. Try to keep the motion of your

nib across the surface as smooth as possible, gliding lightly to build up the tone gradually.

There is a range of shading effects that you can use in place of traditional "smooth" shading. Stippling (the use of dots) and cross-hatching (the use of lines) are equally successful in bringing different tonal values into your work. I recommend practicing these techniques on spare pieces of wood, experimenting with the nib that you select, the way that you hold or apply it to the surface, the temperature setting, and the pressure and duration of the contact. These two techniques enable you to change the shading effect that you are creating through changing the size, shape, frequency, and intensity of the marks. Lighter tones are created by spreading the dots or lines further apart, using a

lighter touch of the nib onto the surface, or reducing the temperature of the machine itself. The opposite approach can be used to create darker and more intense areas of contrasting tone. Practice a range of methods in order to broaden your pyrography "arsenal" of techniques.

Accessories and Equipment

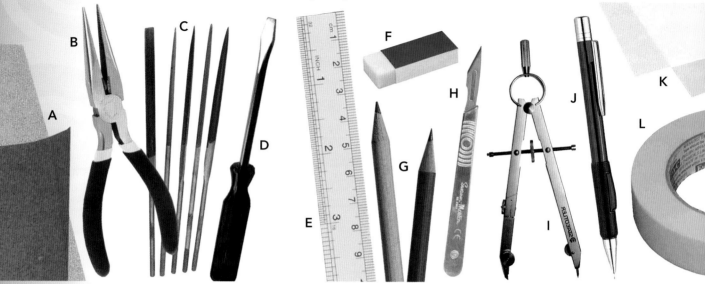

Above: (A) 180- and 240-grit sandpaper; (B) pliers; (C) needle files; (D) screwdriver; (E) ruler; (F) eraser; (G) pencils; (H) craft scalpel/craft knife; (I) pair of compasses; (J) mechanical pencil; (K) tracing paper; (L) masking tape.

There is a range of basic tools that I always advise any pyrographer to have available when working on their designs. Most of these are used for preparing your designs in terms of the layout or the surface itself and are, therefore, equally as vital as your pyrography machine itself. Below is my list of essential items to consider.

If you have built up a varied collection of pyrography pens or nibs, make sure that you invest in a suitable container for safe storage. Pens need to be stored so that the nibs do not get damaged while not in use, and individual nibs should be kept safe in a holder that prevents them from becoming inadvertently misplaced or lost between sessions.

- Pencils, erasers, and sharpeners for drawing out your design. I find mechanical pencils particularly useful for precise work.

- Measuring tools, including a ruler, pair of compasses, circle stencil templates, protractors, and the like, to ensure your designs are accurate where they need to be.

- Access to a laptop or computer with a dual-purpose printer/scanner to help with creating layouts at the correct size and scale for transferring.

- A desk lamp to provide enough light to work by.

- Tracing paper and masking tape to transfer designs that you use from other sources (and to hold them in place as you do so).

- Cutting tools such as a good pair of scissors or a crafts scalpel/craft knife. If you use the latter, invest in a quality cutting mat to protect your worktop.

- Fine grade sandpaper for preparing wooden surfaces or removing marks made in error.

- A selection of hand tools, including screwdrivers, pliers, needle files, and more, for fitting and adjusting nibs in your pyrography machine.

Materials for Use

It is important to keep your pyrography nibs free of the carbon and grit that builds up as you burn. This can easily be achieved by using the edge of a knife blade, scalpel, pair of scissors, or some other sharp blade. Lightly scrape the blade across the surface of the nib to clear the grit. Fine abrasives such as sandpaper can also be used to gently clean nibs, but care must be taken not to use these excessively, as the nibs will wear down more quickly and eventually break. My preferred option is to use a gentler abrasive alternative such as wire wool or the rear of a metal mesh tea strainer, since these do not wear away the nib surface as quickly. One cheap option that is inexpensive and readily available is a kitchen kettle limescale descaler, since these are made of a fine wire wool and are made in small blocks or rings, making them a handy addition to your workspace.

Pyrography can be used across a range of different materials. Wood is the most traditionally suited to the craft, and this is reflected by the wide range of wooden blanks that are available from both physical and online craft supply retailers. I also enjoy identifying and working with a broad spectrum of woodworkers, such as woodturners, frame makers, and the like. There is no greater pleasure than working on something that has been made to your own specifications for a unique project.

Certain woods are better suited for use with pyrography than others. Birch, ash, sycamore, and lime are perfect for pyrography because they have a fine or smooth grain, while also proving a good natural contrast to the burned marks through their pale tone. Some hard woods can be used but present their own different challenges due to their heavier grain; for example, oak has a dense, tough, and dark surface that can be used when creating bold monotone designs but isn't as suitable for delicate lines or soft shading. As well as having a sticky sap residue that bubbles up when burning,

pine can be very tricky to use due to the frequent changes in texture from hard to soft as you move across the grain. This can result in uneven lines or marks where the wood resists the burning in one area before burning exceptionally easily in the next. My simple recommendation when you decide to try a new wood type is to obtain a small offcut to practice on first. This should help you to ascertain whether the material is suited for the purpose that you have in mind before you spend any wasted effort attempting a masterpiece that is ultimately doomed to failure.

Above all else, avoid manmade wooden materials such as MDF, as the glues used to compress the wooden fibers together are extremely toxic when burned. These would be very harmful if you breathe them in while burning a design into the surface. Burning into MDF is no different from burning into a piece of plastic due to the substances used in its creation. There is never any harm in doing some online research first to see if there are any health and safety warnings associated with a specific wood or material.

Leather and canvas can also be used for pyrography with great success. Lighter tones of each are preferable in order to provide a pale surface that allows the burned marks to stand out, but a subtle effect could be achieved with materials in a darker color. Make it a point to use vegetable-tanned leather in place of regular leather since the latter is made with chemicals that are unpleasant and potentially dangerous when burned. Softer materials require a lighter pressure as you work in order to prevent the nib snagging or catching on the surface, which can ruin the quality of your mark making.

Paper, cardstock, and canvas are all cheap and readily available materials for experimentation. The options available in any good art supplier are practically limitless, and the results can be extremely impressive. One obvious benefit of paper over a material such as wood is that you do not need to prepare the surface before working on it. Paper and cardstock can be purchased in a vast range of colors, thicknesses, and textures, giving you a great deal of scope in finding a perfect material for your project in mind. Experimentation in how you combine your woodburning marks in a design with the individual surface qualities of the chosen material can allow you to create some very special and attractive combinations that are enhanced by each other. As previously mentioned, care must be taken to ensure that you do not select any material that involves the use of potentially harmful dyes or chemicals in the manufacturing process.

There are many other materials that are used by pyrographers outside of the more common choices described above. These include (and are not limited to) bark, cork, bone, horn, antlers, and gourds. Each material brings its own individual qualities and challenges, so do your research before using them and see whether they are suitable to achieve whatever idea or concept you have in mind.

Preparing Wood Surfaces

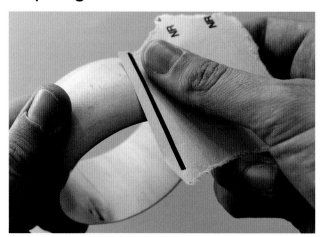

180- to 320-grit sandpaper. The higher the numbered grade of sandpaper, the finer the grit is. Use a coarser sandpaper if the wooden surface requires heavier sanding to prepare it for burning and work your way up through a progression of finer grades to give a smooth finish.

If you are buying readymade craft blanks to burn on, chances are that you will require little to no effort to prepare the surface beforehand. These items are usually finished to a very high standard with smooth surfaces and may be suitable for immediate use. Sheets of birch plywood can also sometimes be ready to work on directly "off the shelf" if they have been made to a high quality.

Most wooden surfaces are best prepared for the application of a pyrography design by being rubbed down with a 180- to 320-grit sandpaper. If you wish, you can use water to slightly dampen the surface between sanding; this allows the grain to raise slightly before the next sanding session and results in a smoother finish. Wet the wood with a damp cloth or similar, allow it to dry, and then sand it again. Repeat this process as many times as you feel necessary to get the required smoothness.

If you are attempting to add a pyrography design to an item that has already been varnished, lacquered, or treated in some way, you will need to remove the finish that has been applied before working on it. Trying to burn through varnishes can create harmful fumes that irritate or damage your respiratory system, as well as generally creating marks that are dirty or messy rather than clean and crisp. Working on items like this may require a more vigorous period of preparation before they can be burned on, such as use of coarser sandpaper or an electric sander.

Completing a Design

People regularly approach me at craft events where I am demonstrating and state that they could never take up pyrography as they are "not artistic enough." I will then demonstrate to them how I use designs that are traced and transferred onto the surface that I am burning. I always tell people that they just need to be able to use a pencil in order to take up and enjoy pyrography, and it is not necessary to be able to create your own designs from scratch. I know many pyrographers who sell their crafts very successfully and work purely from designs that they obtain from a range of sources, rather than creating them from their own imagination. They simply enjoy the process of burning the design into the wood and are extremely skilled in doing so, hence their appeal to paying customers. All you need to be a potentially successful pyrographer is a steady hand and a high degree of patience; everything else about the craft can be learned with time and practice!

Many of my designs are created through freehand drawing or through working on the wood spontaneously to create an idea as I burn. I do regularly design layouts and compositions on my computer using photo editing software, particularly when it comes to anything that involves lettering and text. A computer is a fantastic way to ensure that you get the layout exactly the way you want without having to erase and redraw elements of the composition several times before getting them just right. This also enables you to keep a catalog of your previous designs so that you can easily replicate or adapt a previous work for a new client that wants a personalized version for themselves.

Several of the projects in this book use the process of tracing and transferring to complete an entire design, or specific sections of a composition such as lettering to add a custom message or dedication. I generally use traditional tracing paper in my design work when required to do so, but there are other alternative methods that you could consider using. Graphite or carbon paper can be used as a potential substitute. These sheets are placed under a piece of paper with the design that you intend to transfer so the carbon or graphite marks transfer to the wood as you draw over the source material. The main drawback with these options is the difficulty in removing any excess residue that can sometimes be left on the wooden surface after the burning. As with any tracing technique, it is always best to transfer as few lines as possible in order to prevent having lots of marks that may show through the burning. Only transfer the bare minimum necessary to construct the design that you are creating.

You can never check a design for accuracy too many times. If I'm working on a commission piece, I will send a concept layout to the customer before I start burning so that they can ensure everything is 100% accurate and correct before I start burning it. I will often even let them see the traced or drawn

This house sign had already been completed before the customer realized that "Mara" had been given an extra "R," demonstrating how important it is to check thoroughly before you start burning.

design on the wood prior to using the pyrography machine to give them a second opportunity to look for errors or problems. Fortunately, I've only had a couple of occasions when a mistake has been found after the design had been completed. These included a missing letter from a name and a couple of rogue apostrophes on a frame. Spelling or grammatical errors can turn a fantastic design into a failure; check, check, and check again.

Color and Finishing Treatments

Color can be combined in numerous ways with your pyrography designs to make an array of exciting effects. Various media that are available from all good art and craft retailers, such as watercolor pencils, colored markers, bottled inks, watercolor paints, and the like, are perfect for experimentation. Pyrography marks form a natural barrier of resistance and can prevent the colors of liquid substances from bleeding across into areas that they are not intended for. There are also a wide selection of colored varnishes, paints, and stains on the market that are specifically designed for application to wooden surfaces, and these can add a very exciting dimension to your work. I am particularly fascinated by the different options available that provide an iridescent colored sheen to the wood, as these can look simply beautiful when incorporated into your designs. A number of projects featured within this book use different colored media, so I hope you enjoy trying them as much as I do.

There is a range of methods with which you can protect your design once it is completed. Oils and waxes are particularly suited to designs where you still want to utilize the natural tactile surface qualities of the wood that you are working on. Danish oil is one of my favorite finishing treatments due to the warm luster that it brings out when applied to a wooden surface. I also regularly use a microcrystalline wax, as this protects and polishes the wood when applied in several layers but still feels naturally smooth and soft, making it a pleasure to handle. Beeswax is another treatment that gives a pleasing result.

If you need a tougher and more durable finish to protect your design, there are several varnishes and lacquers available on the market. These can be purchased in matte and gloss effects so that you can find something appropriate for what you have made. Such finishes can be purchased with different application methods to suit the purpose of your work. As well as traditional liquid treatments, spray varnishes can be better suited for irregular surfaces or items where you have applied a color or stain that may be disturbed through the use of a brush. Whichever method you use, ensure that you follow the instructions for that specific type and brand to get the best results, particularly in terms of how to

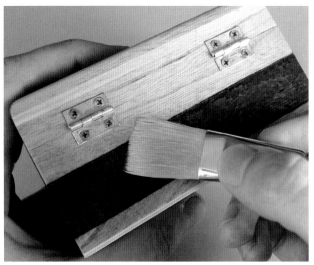

Use a soft, broad paintbrush to apply liquid varnishes or finishes. This will allow you to cover the area smoothly and evenly.

prepare the surface beforehand, how to apply the coats, and how long to leave between layers.

If you are creating a design to be displayed outside or where it will be exposed to strong sunlight, consider using a yacht or marine varnish for maximum protection. Such substances generally contain a UV inhibitor that protects the surface below from the damaging effects of ultraviolet light. Pyrography marks fade when exposed to sunlight, and these finishes can reduce the impact and damage associated with it.

Above all else, the main consideration for any treatment that you choose to apply should be to ensure that it is fit for the intended purpose. Certain varnishes protect the wood from the staining effect of substances that the item's purpose may bring it into contact with, while others are specifically designed to protect items that may be handled extensively or used with food. Do your research carefully and select a finish that does everything that you require.

Chapter 2: Pyrography Projects

Herb Garden Label Set

Patterns on page 154

When you are starting out in pyrography as a new hobby, the progression of your ability to create neat and legible writing is a good indication of your skill level. Everyone knows what the lettering should look like, whether or not they consider themselves creative in any way. If your text is hard to read, poorly spaced, or completely indecipherable, people will, undoubtedly, not hesitate to point that out to you!

Incorporating text into your pyrography designs will therefore help you to see how you are progressing with handling your pyrography pen smoothly and making marks on the wood, as well as allowing you to start considering the basic aspects of the design, such as the layout, composition, and balance in your designs. Working on a simple design brief, like creating a set of wooden herb garden label tags, is an ideal start because it is not too dauntingly complex or excessively ambitious. It does, however, allow you to create something that can be straightforward yet elegant if you make each tag as uniform in appearance as you can manage. This project also allows you to experiment with ways to use your pyrography pen in a decorative yet simple way to make patterned borders. This gives you the opportunity to see what marks you can make that work well visually in combination.

Blank wooden tags like these can be readily purchased from most craft suppliers at a very low cost, which makes them a perfect choice for practicing your woodburning without fear of making mistakes that prove too costly through wasting the blanks. You could also apply the same principles in this project to any project involving small shaped blanks, such as key rings or bookmarks.

Equipment Needed:

- Pyrography machine of your choice and a selection of different pens/nibs

- Set of wooden garden label blanks (as many as you wish to make)

- Pencils, sharpener, and eraser—you can use a mechanical pencil if you prefer

- Tracing paper, scissors, and pliers

- Computer, printer, and paper

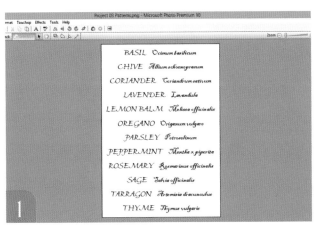

1 Prepare your chosen herb names on your computer at an appropriate size. For my labels, I chose an elegant italic font in capital letters for the common name of each herb, and a more decorative handwritten font in a period style for its Latin translation. Reverse or "flip" the lettering and print a mirror image of the text for ease of tracing and transferring. A more detailed explanation and breakdown of this technique can be found in the Set List Text Art Frame project (page 112).

2 Trace the reversed italic text for one side of one label onto the tracing paper with your pencil. A mechanical pencil can be useful in ensuring that the lines of the lettering are crisp and neat.

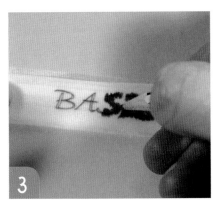

3 Turn the tracing paper over and position it on the label so that the traced italic lettering is in contact with the wooden surface. Scribble on the other side of the paper with a pencil to transfer it onto the wood.

4 Use a fine nib on your pyrography machine, such as a blade or writing nib, on a medium heat setting to neatly burn the lettering into the wood. Position your hand so that you do not accidentally rub off the pencil tracing as you burn. Using a bladed nib will allow you to create crisp, sharp lines.

5 Repeat this process until you have burned the lettering into every wooden label that you are using. Make sure that you keep the spacing and positioning of the words as consistent as possible so that the labels look cohesive as a set.

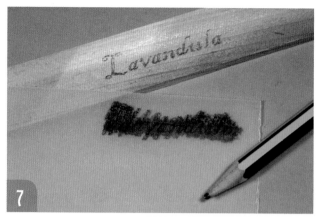

6

Prepare for repeating the process by tracing the reversed handwritten font for the other side of each label onto tracing paper with your pencil. Make sure that you match the correct Latin name with the right label containing the common name already burned into it.

7

Turn the tracing paper over again and position it on the other side of the corresponding label so that the traced lettering is in contact with the wooden surface. Scribble on the other side of the paper again with a pencil to transfer the lettering.

8

Use a spear or writing nib on your pyrography machine at a medium heat to burn the lettering into the wood. You can use a stippled motion if you wish to create a more irregular appearance to contrast with the sharp lines of the italic letters on the other side.

9

Repeat this process again until you have burned the corresponding Latin names into every wooden label. Ensure again that you keep the positioning of the words as even as possible to make the labels as identical as you can.

10

Use a broad shading nib to create an even border around the edge of the label. Press the nib down repeatedly and work your way along the perimeter to form a pattern. Try to keep the spacing of each mark as even as possible so that the pattern is regular in appearance.

11

Repeat the above process using any other nibs that you have available to create a range of different patterned borders. If you are using a nib of looped Nichrome wire, consider altering the shape of it with pliers to make different marks.

Use different combinations of pyrography nibs in sequence to experiment with the creation of new patterns, such as this example where a broad round nib is combined with a triangular impression from a bladed nib to make a new effect.

You can create different variations of patterns by adjusting the way that you apply the nib to the wooden edge. This border was created by increasing and decreasing how much of the nib was brought into contact with the wood, creating an undulating wave of marks in sequence.

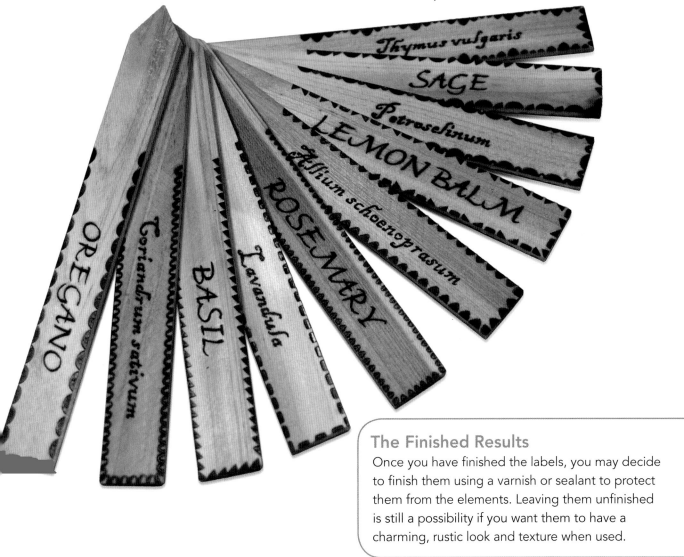

The Finished Results

Once you have finished the labels, you may decide to finish them using a varnish or sealant to protect them from the elements. Leaving them unfinished is still a possibility if you want them to have a charming, rustic look and texture when used.

Engagement Ring Box

Patterns on page 154

Some moments in life are intended to be cherished for all time, and it is a true honor as a craftsperson to be invited to play a part in those treasured moments. The point at which one person asks another to marry them while presenting them with an engagement ring is potentially the most significant and memorable occasion in their lives up to that point. Creating a bespoke memento of that occasion is very special indeed.

Working on such a commission allows you to create something personal and unique, incorporating elements to represent the happy couple: their likes, their character, and the moment itself. Every component of the design should be carefully considered and chosen to fit the design brief that you are working to. There is a wide range of different box styles available to choose from: What shape do they want the box to be? What size do they require? Would they prefer a hinged lid or one that lifts off? You then need to consider any text that they want on the box, including personalized messages or dedications. Careful consideration will need to be given to the details you'll be adding to the design. For example, the person arranging the proposal may not want a specific date added if they are unsure as to when the question will be asked!

In this project, my aim was to create a design on a miniature box that had a jewel-like quality to represent the engagement ring itself. The simple geometric pattern is intended to resemble the facets of a diamond and reflect the contents within. I also chose an elegant and stylish font for the inscription. If necessary, another message or dedication could be added inside the lid or on the base of the box.

Equipment Needed:

- Pyrography machine of your choice and a selection of different pens/nibs
- Small wooden box with lid
- Pencils, sharpener, and eraser—you can use a mechanical pencil if you prefer
- Computer, printer, and paper
- Ruler, masking tape, and tracing paper
- Cardstock and scissors/scalpel
- Miniature decorative metal handle/fixing
- Hand drill and center punch
- Foam/sponge insert (to hold the ring)

1 Cut a strip of paper to confirm the circumference of your round ring box. This is the easiest way to work out sizes for any lettering to be added to your box, or to establish how far certain elements should be spread apart so that they are equally spaced.

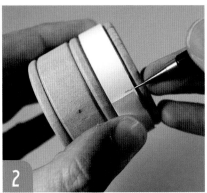

2 Mark off the circumference by wrapping the strip of paper around the box and identify the point where the ends meet with a pencil mark. You can now cut off the excess at one end. If you fold the paper strip in half and then half again, you will be easily able to divide the circumference into quarters.

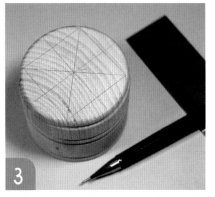

3 Use the quarter markings to divide the round lid into four equal sections with two lines that should be at 90° to each other. Draw a square by joining the ends of these two lines and use the middle of the square's edges to divide the lid into eight even sections.

4 Draw another square using the remaining section markers. Erase all pencil lines so that you are left with just one square on top of another partially visible square. This will form the basis of a diamond design for the box lid.

5 Join four intersections of the initial two squares to form an offset third square at an angle within them. This may sound confusing, but hopefully the picture illustrates how your lid should now look!

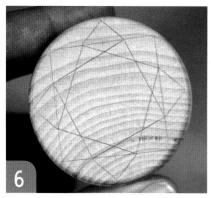

6 Draw another square by joining the four remaining intersections. You should now be left with a border made up of two squares in a star with two identical (but smaller) squares contained within them. This should now resemble the multifaceted structure and appearance of a cut diamond.

7 Add eight lines radiating outward from the points of the two smaller squares to the edge of the lid. Your diamond design is now fully prepared and ready to be burned.

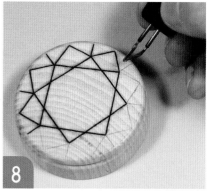

8 Use a fine or bladed nib to neatly go over the pencil lines of the diamond design. Try to keep these as straight and as sharp as possible; this will help give your lid a precise and well-defined structure in keeping with the nature of the design.

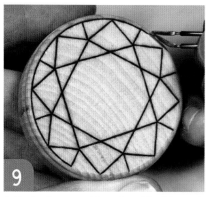

9 Add a border around the edge of the lid, neatly joining all the points together with a circle. Hold the box securely while doing this since small items are tricky to work on and a firm grip is essential to avoid injury.

10 Start shading the central elements of the diamond design using a small spoon point nib on a low heat setting. Work over the surface slowly and carefully to keep the tone as smooth and even as possible.

11 Turn the temperature of the pyrography machine up slightly and start to shade the next segments of the design, working outward from the center and the areas already filled in. You are aiming for a tone that is slightly darker. Build up the shading in gradual layers until you are happy with the result.

12 Raise the temperature setting again slightly and begin shading every other element on the outer ring of the diamond design. This needs to be another tonal step darker than the previous sections so that you continue to add dimension to the design.

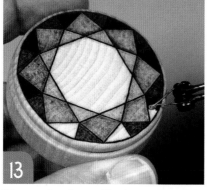

13 When you turn the machine temperature dial up for these final sections, you should be at a medium-high setting that creates a deeper shadow area when you shade the outlined areas. This completes the simple yet effective diamond pattern on your lid.

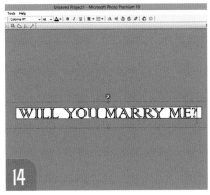

14 Use your photo editing software to prepare a template for the text to be added around the lid. The height of the template should be the height of the side of the lid, and the width should be the circumference of the box. Select a stylish and elegant font for your inscription.

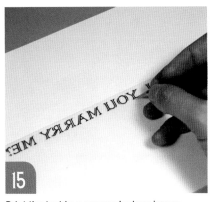

15 Print the text in a reversed mirror image format and trace the lettering onto tracing paper with a sharp pencil. Alternatively, you could use a mechanical pencil due to their precision. Make sure that you trace the lettering as neatly as possible so that the inscription is well defined when transferred.

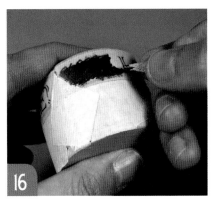

16 Secure the tracing paper as firmly as possible with masking tape so that it stays in place on the curved surface of the box. Transfer the lettering onto the box by scribbling on the reverse side of the tracing paper, and then remove it carefully to avoid smudging the pencil marks.

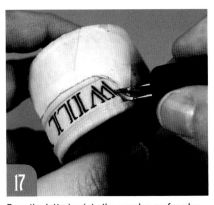

17 Burn the lettering into the wooden surface by using a fine or bladed nib at a low temperature setting. Use the tip of the nib carefully to ensure that any distinct points or fine lines are created as crisply as possible. Allowing the blade to gently cut into the surface helps to keep the lines sharp and straight.

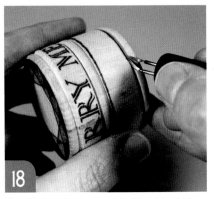

18 Now that you have completed the lid, add two parallel tramlines around the top and bottom of the box itself. These will be used to form a decorative border panel running around the whole of the box compartment.

19 Mark off eight equal measurements on the strip of paper you used to mark the circumference. Wrap this around the box compartment and use the pencil to divide the circumference into eight identical sections.

20 Use the corners and middle points of each section to make a star pattern. Placing a ruler on a small curved surface is tricky, so use the straight edge of a piece of cardstock to join the points together with a pencil. The cardstock can be held around the curved surface as a flexible ruler.

21 Burn the lines into the wood using a fine or bladed nib at a low temperature setting. This uses an identical approach to that used to burn the diamond design into the lid. Work slowly and carefully due to the size of the small box and hold it firmly to prevent any slips.

22

Carefully shade the segments of the star shapes to add definition. Use a small shading nib, such as a spoon point, and take advantage of the lip of the nib to shade into any acute angles in the patterns.

23

Apply different tones to the star patterns by adjusting the temperature or building up darker layers of tone. Continue the shading on every individual panel around the box compartment so that they are all shaded in an identical fashion.

24

Lightly use a center punch to mark the very middle of the lid. Drill a hole through the point indicated and fit the miniature decorative handle securely through it. Tighten the fitting as much as possible so that it doesn't work itself loose.

25

Cut your piece of foam or sponge to fit inside the box. If you cut it slightly bigger than the internal size of the box compartment, the foam should expand to stay in place more securely once inside. A slot cut in the middle of the foam can then be used to hold the ring securely within the box.

The Finished Results

Your engagement ring box is now ready for the big day . . . Hopefully your hard work and effort in creating such a beautiful design will result in a resounding "Yes!" for the person behind the proposal. Miniature items can be very rewarding to create, but the small scale brings its own challenges for you to overcome.

Texture Print Key Fobs

Patterns on page 155

As a child, I collected key rings for many years, buying them at any locations or tourist spots that I visited as well as receiving many from friends and family after they had been away. My house must have appeared positively full of them! The endless appeal of shiny things must have contributed to this desire and even now, my household keys have various key fobs that remind me of special events and trips. The only potential spanner in the works is the growing size of the bunch of keys, as some people say that it can now be regarded as a deadly weapon. I have now vowed to stop adding to the growing collection, so problem solved (with a little perseverance).

Key fobs are an extremely popular choice of item to make for all crafters, including pyrographers. Wooden fob blanks can be obtained in a wide range of shapes and sizes, and it is also possible to buy vegetable-tanned leather key fob blanks that are suitable for burning designs into. They can be tailored in terms of the decorative theme to suit all occasions and are easy to personalize, which makes

them an ideal choice for a special gift. They are usually supplied in bundles of several blanks rather than as individual items, which means that they are also an affordable choice for a budding newcomer to any craft.

As with any small creation, a beautifully decorated key fob is a challenge for the maker and an extremely tempting potential purchase for a customer. Key fobs are among the items that I would term as "pocket money" designs. They are not expensive and, therefore, are highly likely to be an affordable impulse buy if you have them on sale at a craft fair. People like to browse through an array of small items and will often consider buying a design that appeals to them or reflects their personality. You may even be asked to personalize an existing creation with an initial or name to make it even more unique to the buyer; that is one reason why designs with an initial on them, such as in this project, are an exciting challenge to any crafter.

Equipment Needed:

- Pyrography machine of your choice and a selection of different pens/nibs
- Computer, printer, and paper
- Pencils, sharpener, and eraser—you can use a mechanical pencil if you prefer
- Tracing paper, masking tape, and scissors/scalpel
- Quantity of wooden key fob blanks with appropriate split rings

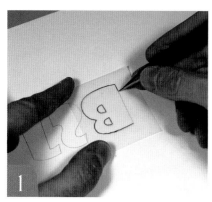
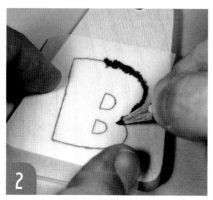
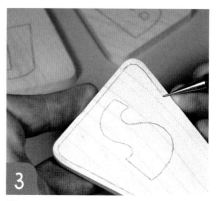

1. Print your chosen font at a size that is appropriate for the wooden blanks that you are using, and trace the selected initial using a pencil onto a piece of tracing paper. Make sure that the letter is big enough to be clearly visible while still leaving enough space around it for the pattern.

2. Position the tracing paper on one side of the wooden blank with the drawn letter in contact with the surface. Use masking tape to hold it in position securely if needed. Scribble on the reverse side firmly to transfer the letter onto the wood (without pressing too hard, as this may dent the surface.)

3. After repeating the above process for the quantity of blanks that you plan to decorate, add a running border around the side of the fob by holding a pencil in a fixed position and moving the fob around against a specific fingertip. Rotating the fob carefully in this way creates an evenly spaced line.

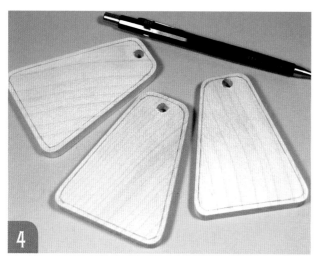

4. Repeat the previous process to complete an identically spaced borderline on the plain reverse side of the fob. Try to make sure that each line is similar in terms of spacing so that you create a design with consistency in appearance.

5. Cut a piece of tracing paper so that it is slightly larger than the fob itself and mark out in pencil the edge of the border you have drawn. This will ensure that you only trace what you need when working on the pattern that you have chosen to apply.

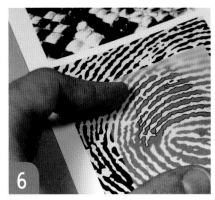

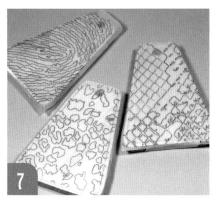

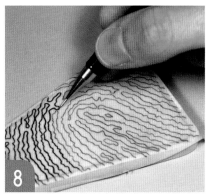

6 Flip the tracing paper over and place it on the chosen pattern that you have printed. Start to trace the structure of the pattern in pencil so that it can be transferred onto the wooden blank. Keep your lines crisp and neat by using a mechanical pencil or a very sharp regular pencil.

7 Repeat the same process for all the fobs that you are making, securing them in place with masking tape. I used three different patterns in the example pictured, namely a fingerprint, leopard print, and snakeskin design. You can make each fob unique or use the same pattern across the whole set.

8 Place the traced pattern design facedown on the plain side of your wooden fob and carefully draw over the lines to replicate the pattern exactly on the surface. Use this method rather than scribbling since the tracing paper will be used again on the other side of the fob.

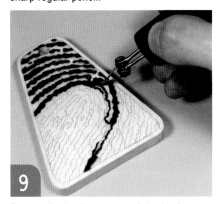

9 Remove the tracing paper and start to burn the first pattern into the wood. For the fingerprint pattern, use a finely pointed nib such as a spear at a medium temperature setting to burn the irregular lines of each ridge in the pattern. Try to stay within your traced lines at all times.

10 Flip the tracing paper again so that you are now transferring the side you drew on most recently onto the wooden surface. This will create a mirror image of the pattern that you have just burned. Scribble on the rear to transfer the marks over, but do not go past the border or letter outline.

11 Once you have transferred the whole pattern, repeat the same process of burning on this side of the fob with the same nib to create an identical appearance. Do not cross the pencil outlines of the letter or border in order to keep the wood free from any burn marks.

Repeat the same process of tracing and transferring for any other patterns that you are using onto their respective blanks. For the leopard print pattern, start by tracing the dark spots of the design, as these will give you the main structure of the texture that you are creating.

13 Use the spear or bladed nib at a medium setting to burn the spots of the leopard print pattern. Build up a textured feel by making a series of marks in a similar direction; this will help to create the impression of fur. Refer to your source image for help if needed to recreate the selected pattern.

14 Repeat the same process on the main side of the blank of transferring the mirror image of the pattern once you have finished burning the first side. Remember to stay within the lines that you have drawn to create the border and the initial itself.

15 Use the same approach to the burning on the side with the letter as you did on the reverse in order to reproduce a consistent design and texture. Do not burn over the outline of the letter or the borderline so that these stay neatly defined and clear of any inadvertent burning.

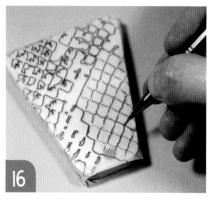
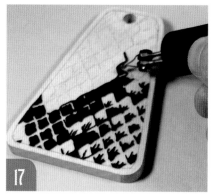

16 The snakeskin pattern is one of the more complex textures to recreate. Draw on the reverse side of the tracing paper carefully in order to transfer the areas that will represent the darkest shadows and tones. Try not to miss any lines at all, as this may make the burning stage more difficult.

17 Use a spoon point nib on a medium to high temperature setting to fill in the areas of shadow. This texture is smoother in visual appearance than the leopard fur, so use the bowl of the nib for larger areas of flat tone. The lip of the nib can be used for any finer details or lines.

18 Use a fine or bladed nib to add the finest lines of the snakeskin scales as you build up the definition of the pattern. A medium temperature setting on the pyrography machine should be perfect. Keep the lines as neat and crisp as possible, rotating the wooden blank as you work if needed.

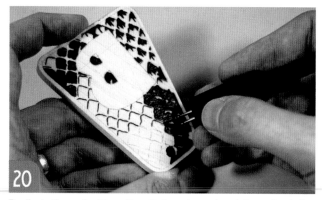

19 Flip the tracing paper again, secure it in place with masking tape, and transfer the pattern onto the side with the initial, remembering to keep the border and letter free of any pencil marks by scribbling around and within the lines that you have already drawn on the wood.

20 Replicate the snakeskin pattern that you have already burned onto the plain side of the wooden blank, using the same burning techniques with the same nibs to give a matching visual appearance that is as identical as possible. Keep the letter itself and the border free from any burning at all.

Use a small shading nib such as a spoon point on a low to medium heat setting to add shading to the fingerprint pattern between each dark ridge. Work slowly and carefully across the surface to keep the shaded tone as even and consistent as possible, keeping the border as crisp and neat as you can.

Repeat the same process of shading on the side with the initial on it, shading within the ridges of the fingerprint pattern but keeping the letter and border free from any shading. You can now appreciate the contrast between the burned and unburned areas of wood that create the chosen design.

For the leopard print pattern, use a fine or bladed nib on a low temperature setting to add more definition to the fur between the darker spots. If you follow the source image as closely as possible in terms of the "direction" of the lines, you will start to build up a realistic visual texture.

Repeat the same process on both sides of the leopard print fob. Use repeated short lines with the point of the fine nib to recreate the feel of the short fur of the leopard, reflecting the direction as accurately as possible from the image you used to replicate the pattern as best as you can.

Use a small shading nib on a low temperature setting to add areas of shading to the snakeskin pattern. Follow the source image for reference and apply shading to the lighter areas of tone, flicking the nib up from the surface as you work to create a graduated fading effect where needed.

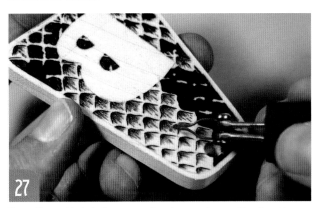

Complete the same process on the side of the snakeskin fob containing the letter that you have drawn out, taking great care to leave the initial itself and the surrounding border free from any shading.

Use a fine or bladed nib on a medium temperature setting to add linear detail to your snakeskin pattern over the top of the shading that you have created previously. Look at the source pattern to guide you in this, adding detail where needed to help build up the pattern you are creating.

28

Use the point of a fine or bladed nib at a medium temperature setting to add any outstanding linear definition. Irregular lines can help to give a textured shading effect across the top of each scale in the pattern, as well as emphasizing the negative space between each.

29

Once the textural burning is completed on each key fob, remove any remaining visible lines with an eraser so that no pencil marks can be seen. If you wish, finish each fob with a protective oil or wax before attaching the split ring through the pre-drilled holes.

The Finished Results

Your fobs are now ready for use or sale! The scope of decoration that you can create for a range of key fobs is limited only by your imagination. Due to their small size, it can be quite easy to build up a substantial stock of decorative key fobs as you become more confident and proficient in your craft.

Mandala~esque Table Set

Pattern on page 156

In recent years, there has been a massive surge in popularity for "adult" coloring books, designed to promote relaxation and calmness by encouraging us to take a step away from our busy daily lives and into the activities we enjoyed as children. These books are available in many themes, but I have always been the most drawn to the beauty of the books featuring mandala designs. These elegant, exquisite patterns are a joy to admire and provide an ideal challenge for any craftsperson to incorporate into their work.

If you so wished, you could trace and transfer a mandala design onto a wooden surface to burn; however, that would be a challenge due to the complexity and the level of detail involved. There is an alternative option available to you, and that is to create your own version of a mandala from scratch.

This may sound like a daunting prospect at first, but my aim in this project is to show you that it is not as difficult as you may think.

Because this was an unplanned mandala design, you won't find a template in this book for this project. What you see in these photos was not planned and simply evolved as I created the design in a natural and spontaneous manner. I did not know what the pattern would look like when I started; I allowed the design to develop gradually in segments, which resulted in a unique and complex design. You can recreate this design that I have made here if you wish to better understand and apply the process, but you can also use the same technique of working outward symmetrically from a central point to create your own unique mandala-esque motif.

Equipment Needed:

- Pyrography machine of your choice and a selection of different pens/nibs
- Quantity of wooden placemat blanks (as many as you wish to make)
- Quantity of wooden coaster blanks (one per placemat)
- Pencils, sharpener, and eraser—you can use a mechanical pencil if you prefer
- Ruler, protractor, circle template, and compasses
- Assorted items or blanks to draw around
- Tracing paper

Draw a fine border of ⅛" to ³⁄₁₆" (3 to 4mm) around the edge of each placemat or coaster using a pencil and ruler. This will act as a frame for the decoration that you are about to create and gives your work a more polished and professional appearance. Measure the lines as accurately as possible for neatness.

Create the outline of the frame using a fine or bladed nib on a low-medium temperature. Keep your lines as smooth as possible and try to ensure that they continue fluidly whenever you stop and reposition your nib to give the most precise finish that you can achieve.

Carefully block each frame in using a fine shading nib such as a small spoon point. Work along the inside of each line meticulously and slowly so as not to ruin the frame itself by going over at any point. Try to create an even and smooth dark tone.

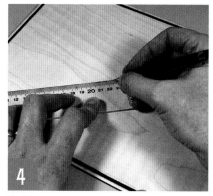

Find the center point of the placemats by placing your ruler diagonally across from opposite corners and marking where they intersect in the middle. This will form the starting point for your mandala on the placemats, while the coasters will feature an identical partial design radiating from a corner.

Mark up your placemat using a pencil, ruler, and protractor so that you have 12 equal 30° sections radiating from the central point. The coasters will feature a quarter of the same design, so ensure that you have three equally measured 30° sections radiating from one chosen corner.

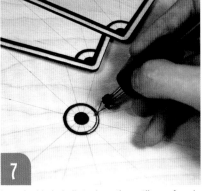

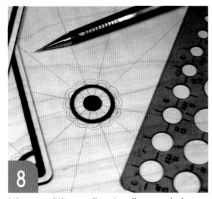

6

You can develop your design in any way that you like to make it unique and spontaneous, so these steps are a description of how I created this pattern. I started with several rings drawn around the central point with a circle template, replicating the same pattern on the coasters.

7

I used a bladed nib to draw the outlines of each ring or circle and a small spoon point nib to add dark shading to the ring. A whole circle was then created in the middle of the placemats, with a quarter of the same pattern beginning to emerge on the matching coasters.

8

I then used the smaller stencils on a circle template to work my way around between each radiating spoke I had drawn on all items, using two different sizes to build up a section of the pattern that reminded me of the petals of a flower.

9

I then went over the petal shapes with a bladed nib at a low-medium temperature to burn them crisply into the wooden surface of all items. Working on each item in turn at every stage meant that the pattern I was developing was the same, building up a coherent visual link between each one.

10

Next, I decided to add some linear detail to the central circle, adding some straight and curved lines in a manner that also created a more distinct flower pattern in the middle section. This idea was a spur-of-the-moment decision; this pattern was not planned in any way and evolved as I worked.

11

Finding items to draw around can add a whole new dimension to a design. I found a star blank on my desk (left over from the reversi game project on page 141) and traced around one section on each of the 12 spokes in pencil to extend the design as I gradually worked my way out from the central point.

12

I went around each outline of the newly drawn star section with a bladed nib before dividing them in half with a line down the spoke. I then shaded each alternate half to add shadow and definition to the design. The same process was also transferred across to the pattern on the coasters.

Mandala-esque Table Set   43

Further use of the circle templates resulted in the creation of six "petals" around the twelve spokes. These were decorated by breaking them up into small sections with straight lines, which, again, was an unplanned decision that arose as I worked on the surfaces.

Drawing a single new element and then tracing it for easier repetition is another way in which you can extend your design quickly and efficiently. I drew a single leaf shape between two spokes and then repeated it quickly all the way around by using tracing paper to repeat it exactly.

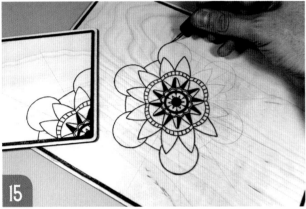

The design was then extended through the use of the larger stencils in a circle template and drawing a circle between them with a pair of compasses from the central point. Sharp outlines for each were completed using the fine bladed nib at a low-medium temperature.

These large elements were then filled with decorative patterns to fit the available space appropriately. A series of concentric rings were added to the large circles in a ripple effect using a circle template, while the leaves were decorated with hand-drawn swirling lines.

At this stage, I started to draw more intricate elements that were then traced and transferred around the design to expand it in a more dynamic manner. Some parts were drawn by hand, while other sections that were circular utilized a circle template for accuracy and neatness.

I added a few small circles and teardrop shapes on several spokes, as they gave the impression of decorative beads or similar. I then continued to add these outlines using a bladed nib so that the design was crisp and precise across all the placemats and coasters.

The outer edge of the protractor and a fine pencil line proved to be a very quick and easy way of "joining" spokes that were far apart. This goes to show how sometimes you can be inspired by whatever is available at hand as you work, with no planning or forethought involved.

I used a series of neat dots in a row using a ballpoint writing nib along the lines I had just drawn with the protractor edge. I decided to do this because it gave the impression of a fine beaded chain, fitting in nicely with the impression of jeweled beads I had selected to use previously.

At this point, I decided that the structure of the design had now reached as far as I wanted it to. I went back over the placemats and coasters with an eraser to remove any remaining pencil marks before I could move onto adding the final shading and decoration.

Using a small spoon point nib, I went back through the design to add bold, dark shading to some of the forms I had created, particularly the intricate leaf and bead designs. I worked carefully to ensure that whatever I shaded on the first placemat was then exactly replicated on all other items.

The temperature setting on the pyrography machine was then reduced in order to add some lighter tones of shading across the design. This was a successful way to start adding definition and contrast across the design by making certain areas stand out against those surrounding them.

24 Darker shades of tone were used to continue building up the contrast within the design. I also added other patterns into the design, such as the fish scale effect between the swirling leaves. This was added quickly using the circle template before being shaded to enhance the visual effect.

25 A few final finishing touches were then added in the form of some additional linear detail at points where I felt something was lacking. Sometimes it is helpful to just sit back and look at the design with a critical eye to see if it meets your expectations or whether more work is still necessary.

The Finished Results

It's very rare to start work on a design with absolutely no preconceived ideas as to how it will turn out, but you can see from this project that it can be a rewarding and enjoyable experience. You could start a project in this manner countless times and no two end results would be the same.

Celtic Knotwork Bangle

Patterns on page 157

Celtic knotwork is one of my favorite themes for use in my pyrography designs. The scope of visual appearance is almost infinite in range, from the simplest basic knot motifs right up to extremely complicated patterns that almost baffle the eye due to the detail involved. I find Celtic knotwork very relaxing to create; there is something calmly reassuring about the way that the lines intersect and overlap. Of course, this does also mean that it can be very easy to make mistakes with just a single line crossing at the wrong point resulting in the whole design being ruined if you know where to look!

Wooden bangle blanks can sometimes be more difficult to source in terms of the numbers of suppliers that stock them, but they are available if you do your research (particularly online). They can often be found in a range of styles, shapes, and sizes, and are often sold for use with other crafts, such as decoupage and painting, in addition to pyrography.

To add something a little different to this project, I used a solid point pyrography machine that also has the capacity to be used as a heated craft tool for the application of metallic foil to various surfaces. This allowed me to enhance the textured surface of the bangle with gold highlights, giving it a bit more "bling" as the curved form glitters and sparkles when looked at from different angles. This experiment was great fun and really added an exciting new element to the pyrography design. As the metallic foils are available in a range of colors, the possibilities of what you can achieve are only limited by the scope of your imagination. Why not get some and give it a try?

Equipment Needed:

- Pyrography machine of your choice and a selection of different pens/nibs

- Wooden bangle blank(s)

- Pencils, sharpener, and eraser—you can use a mechanical pencil if you prefer

- Scissors and circle template

- Scrap paper

- Gold heat foil (and a solid point pyrography machine or similar craft kit to apply it)

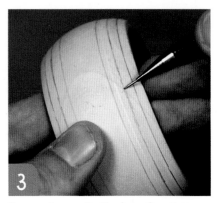

Draw two parallel lines around the surface of your bangle. Drawing straight lines on a curved surface can be tricky. My tip is to place the pencil on an item at the correct height on a flat surface, bring the pencil in contact with the wooden bangle, and then slowly rotate the blank to draw a line. You can then turn the bangle over and do the same from the other side to create your parallel marks.

Adding another item (such as a wooden coaster) under the object with the pencil on top means that you can create two more lines nearer to the edge of the bangle by repeating the same process again. You now have two pairs of pencil tramlines, one on each side of the bangle's surface.

You can also use the tip of your fingers as a rough running guide to add a third line in the middle of each pair. Keep your hand in a fixed position and hold the pencil steady while turning the bangle around against your fingertips from each side; you should now have three parallel lines on each side.

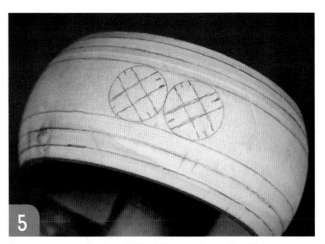

Use a circle template to draw two circles within the central band of the bangle. Both circles should touch each other as well as touching the lines immediately above and below them. We will use these to create a basic Celtic knot pattern without the need to trace or copy from another source.

Draw two crosses in the middle of the two circles. The distance between the lines should be roughly the same as that between the first pair of lines immediately above or below the circles, since these will join up as part of the knotwork. Lines at different distances will make the knotwork uneven.

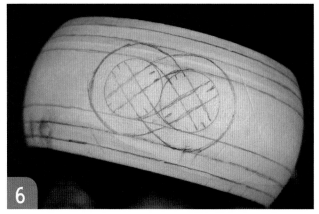

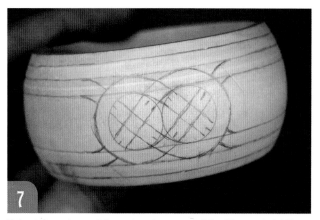

Extend the innermost lines of each cross so that they loop around the circle opposite them. Use the first tramlines above and below to help get the dimensions similar. You should now be able to make out a distinctive "figure of eight" motif that will form the basis of our knot design.

Extend the outermost lines of each cross past the "figure of eight" so that they join up smoothly with the nearest row of tramlines. We have now established the basic drawn structure of the complete Celtic knot to be burned into our bangle. I promise you that it will all become clearer as you start to burn it!

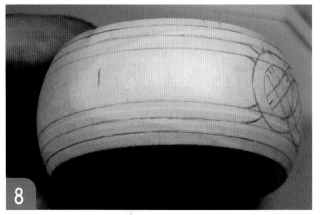

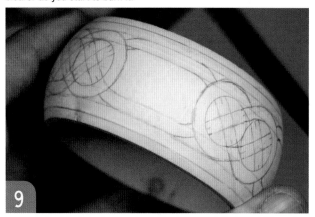

Use a strip of scrap paper to work out the bangle circumference. Cut it to size, fold it in half, and then in half again. Wrap the paper around the center of the bangle with the ends at the center of the two circles. Mark off at every fold with a pencil line, and you will have evenly placed three more knot designs!

Repeat steps 4 to 7 again three more times, starting at each point by drawing two identical circles on either side of the points that you just marked from the strip of paper. You should now have drawn a total of four identical Celtic knots at regular intervals around a curved bangle . . . easy, eh?

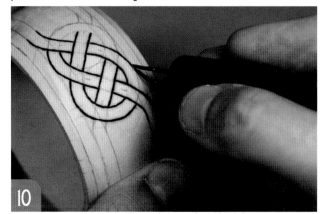

Use a fine or bladed nib at a low-medium temperature setting and start to finalize the lines of your Celtic knot. Remember the basic principle that each section should go over one line and then under the next before repeating the process. Draw more lines or erase unnecessary ones if it helps you better visualize how the design should look once burned.

Repeat the process for each of the four Celtic knots you have drawn around the bangle and gradually join the whole design together into a single flowing pattern. Crisp lines with no incorrect overlaps are the key to good knotwork, so take your time and think before each touch of the hot pyro nib.

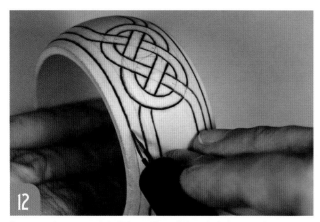

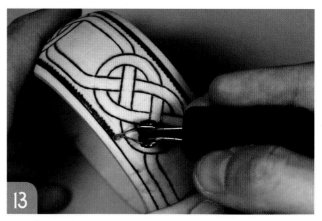

Once you have completed the outline of the whole knotwork pattern, burn the remaining outermost line of the three parallel marks we initially created on each side of the bangle with a fine or bladed nib. This will form part of the border for the textured area to be created around the Celtic pattern.

Use a fine shading nib, such as a small spoon point, at a medium-high temperature setting to build up a dark shaded border along the inside of each tramline nearest to the edge of the bangle. Work your way slowly and carefully along both sides until the shaded areas are joined up and complete.

Use the same fine shading nib at the same temperature setting to add a similar shaded border around the outside of the entire Celtic knotwork pattern. Take extra care when shading into any acute angles or within small areas so that you don't ruin the sharp lines of the pattern.

Use a broad shading nib at a medium-high heat setting to start adding a dappled texture to all the areas surrounding the knotwork itself. Keep the marks evenly spaced but with a few areas of unburned wood still visible to enhance the sensation of a roughly hewn texture to emulate stone or something to that effect.

Change to a finer shading nib of a smaller size and add another layer of dappled marks over the top of what you just created. The smaller nib will result in a darker, more intense mark at the same heat setting as the larger nib and will, therefore, increase the layered texture that you are building up.

Use a fine or bladed nib at a low-medium heat setting to add some more detail to the bands of the knotwork itself. A few light flashes running away from the lines at right angles from the point where they cross over another line will add to the sense of definition and depth in the design.

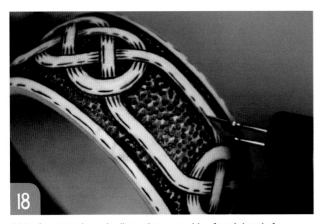

Add a few more irregular lines along one side of each band of knotwork. These don't need to be precise or measured in any way; they merely act to add more substance to each line and emphasize the fact that the bands are flowing around the bangle above the textured background surface.

And now for the fun! Use the solid point pyrography machine to apply the gold foil to the textured area of the bangle. Hold the foil against the bangle and press the hot pen down to transfer the gold onto the wood. Make random scribbled marks on top of the textured area so that the gold foil forms various highlights across the rough surface of the burned marks. Stick to the areas between the knotwork so that the hints of gold provide a striking contrast with the pattern itself.

The Finished Results

Once you've started experimenting with adding hot foil to your pyrography designs, I guarantee that you will want to try more ideas in no time at all. The hot foil is available in a multitude of metallic colors, making it a fascinating technique to combine with your assorted projects and commissions.

Art Nouveau Wall Organizer

Patterns on page 157

One challenge that I always find enjoyable as a crafter is to create a design in homage to a renowned style or movement. This is a rewarding way that you can stretch yourself creatively as a designer by attempting to work to a goal you have set yourself in successfully honoring a recognizable theme that will be very apparent once completed. The sources of inspiration are literally endless, so you will have no trouble finding something to inspire you.

The Art Nouveau movement is one such style that I have always found appealing due to its richly ornate decoration. It is characterized by its use of natural forms and flowing curves, which were applied to art, jewelry making, textiles, and architecture, as well as graphic, interior, and product design. I have always been particularly drawn to the elaborate ironwork frequently seen in the "Metro" underground railway stations of Paris, so I decided to create a design that emulates their bold and elegant appearance using pyrography.

As I wanted to create something a little different for this project, I decided to create my own wall organizer to hang keys or coats while also acting as a safe place for smaller possessions to prevent them from getting lost or misplaced. I selected a large wooden plaque along with some antique brass hooks and nameplates to add to the vintage feel of the design. I also found a blank wooden tray with a shaped edge that reminded me of the Art Nouveau style, deciding that half of the tray would form a perfect shelf compartment for the piece. A few minutes of careful sawing later and all was ready for action! If you don't have access to a tray blank, you could always consider a suitably sized wooden box to use for the shelf in this project.

- Pyrography machine of your choice and a selection of different pens/nibs
- Large wooden plaque
- Wooden tray or box, preferably with a shaped decorative edge
- Masking tape, wood glue, and cotton swabs
- Antique brass hooks and screw fixings
- Antique brass nameplates and screw fixings
- Pencils, sharpener, and eraser—you can use a mechanical pencil if you prefer
- Computer, scanner/printer, and paper
- Screwdriver, sandpaper, handsaw, and hand drill
- Tracing paper and masking tape
- Thick white cardstock, ruler, scissors/scalpel, and cutting mat

Mark out the required section of your wooden tray or box blank that will form the shelf compartment of your design. Use a pencil and ruler to prepare the line that you will cut along. If you work carefully, one tray or box can be used to make shelves for two separate projects.

Use an appropriate saw to cut your tray or box along the line that you have marked out. As many such blanks are often made of a soft material like basswood, a simple handsaw is perfectly adequate; a power tool would be more likely to damage the wood. Support the item as you cut it.

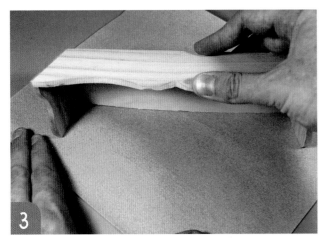

Place a piece of fine sandpaper on a flat surface and carefully sand the cut edge of the tray or box to make the surface as flat and smooth as possible. This will ensure that the shelf fits perfectly against the surface of the plaque when it is attached for maximum contact.

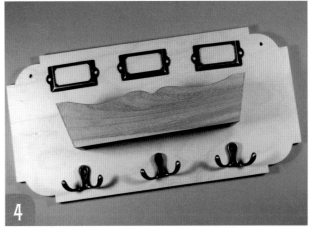

Place your newly cut shelf on the plaque along with the hooks and nameplates that you plan to use. This gives you the opportunity to plan the approximate composition and spacing of the design before you start to draw or burn on the wooden surface.

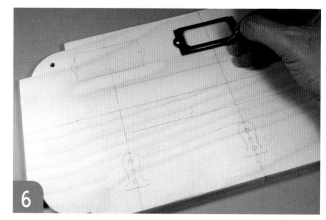

Use a pencil and ruler to plan out the exact placing and dimensions of your design. This will help you to plan a design that is evenly laid out with precise measurements between each component. An effective design can succeed or fail on the accuracy of the preparation completed at this stage!

Drawing around the nameplates and hooks lightly in pencil will help you to understand exactly where each will be placed once fixed to the plaque. This will also help you avoid inadvertently spending time burning an area that is then covered up once a fixing is added.

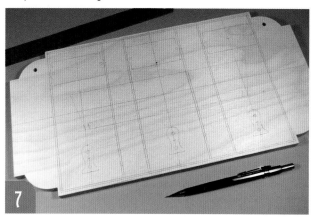

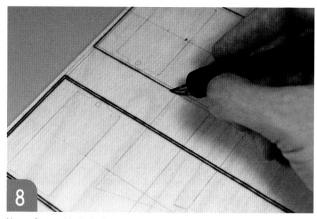

Draw out a series of identical borders using parallel pencil lines with a ruler to create three separate but identical panels around each hook and nameplate. This helps to add definition and structure to the composition, around which the decorative details will be added.

Use a fine or bladed nib on a medium temperature setting to burn each crisp outline of the three panels you have drawn. Keep the lines as sharp as you can and try to make sure that they meet neatly at each corner without crossing over in error.

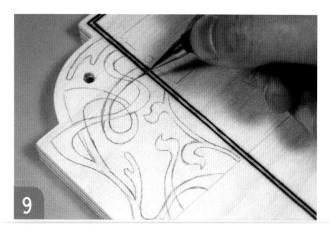

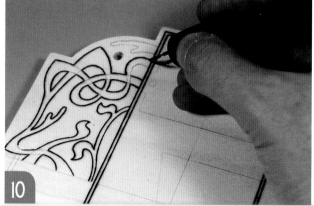

Design your own Art Nouveau decoration at one end of the wooden plaque, working up from a pencil line that marks the exact halfway point of the surface area. Use images from books or the Internet if you need a reference point to work from, or draw freely if you feel able to do so.

Use the fine or bladed nib again at the same temperature setting to draw the outlines of your Art Nouveau decorative feature. Once completed, this section will now form the basis of your design by being replicated around the rest of the plaque, creating your own symmetrical border pattern.

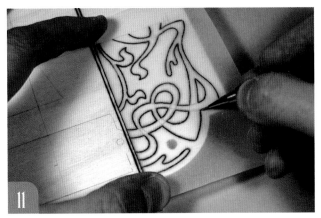

Cut a piece of tracing paper to size and carefully trace the section of design that you have just burned. Make sure that the traced lines are as accurate as possible so that the section to be transferred matches the existing lines burned into the wood exactly; this will ensure the symmetry of your design.

Flip the piece of tracing paper over and position it onto the wooden surface on the other side of the halfway line so that it lines up precisely with the burned design. Use masking tape to hold the tracing paper in position if necessary.

Draw over the design accurately and neatly with a pencil in order to transfer the other half of the design onto the wood. Try not to press too hard, as this can leave an indentation in the wood itself. Keep the tracing paper as tidy as possible, as it will be used twice more before you finish with it.

Remove the tracing paper and check that the design has transferred as fully as possible. If you wish, you can draw over the transferred lines in pencil to make sure that they do not rub off as you work. Marks transferred from tracing paper are prone to smudging if you wipe or rub them accidentally.

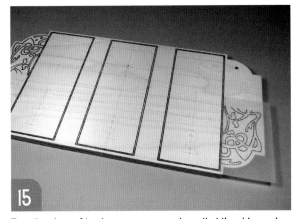

Turn the piece of tracing paper over again so that the side you have most recently drawn on is now facing downward. Place it carefully in position against the panel border and halfway line at the opposite end of the plaque ready for the third section of the design to be marked out.

Repeat the tracing and transferring process at the opposite end of the plaque to complete the third and fourth sections of the design so that both ends are fully prepared. Burn over all of the newly transferred sections using a fine or bladed nib until all of the design segments are completed.

Draw out a similar pattern in an Art Nouveau style between two of the main panels on one side of the halfway line. Make it as similar as possible to the existing patterns at each end so that the design looks consistent. You can use traced sections of the previous pattern to help with this if you wish.

Trace the new pattern and repeat the transferring process three more times to replicate the pattern fully between all three central panels. You can rotate or flip the design in any way that you wish to position it. Your design is now starting to join up completely and is ready to be burned into the wood.

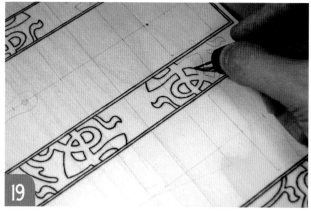

Use the fine or bladed nib to continue the crisp outlines around each newly traced and transferred section of the pattern. Rotate or reposition the piece of wood as you work if this makes it easier for you to follow the flowing lines of the design. Make sure your hand can move freely in order to burn.

Once the outlines are completed, change your pyrography pen to a small shading nib—such as a fine spoon point—and turn the temperature up to a medium-high setting. You can now start to carefully shade between the border outlines, creating an even, dark tone to give the impression of ironwork.

Continue to shade your way all around each of the panel borders and the various sections of Art Nouveau adornment. Take care to shade carefully within the relevant outlines in order to keep your design as sharp and crisp as possible. Patience and a steady hand will win the day!

Use a broad shading nib at a high temperature setting to add a darkly shaded edge to the top of your shelf compartment. This is a particularly effective technique when the edge concerned is shaped, as it gives extra definition to your design. Press lightly so that you do not burn deeply into the wood.

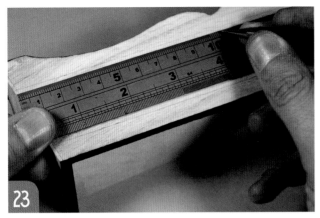

Use a pencil and ruler to measure and mark out two parallel pairs of tramlines as a border for the decorative text that will be added to the shelf compartment. Only draw these marks lightly in pencil, particularly if the item is made of a softer material, such as basswood or lime.

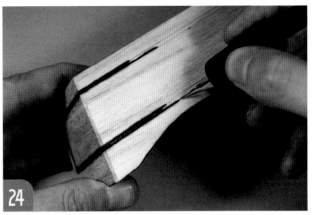

Use a fine or bladed nib—set at a medium heat temperature—to carefully draw and fill both parallel tramlines on the shelf compartment. Work carefully and ensure that you have a firm grip on the item you are burning. It is easy for unusual shapes to slip or move if they are not well supported.

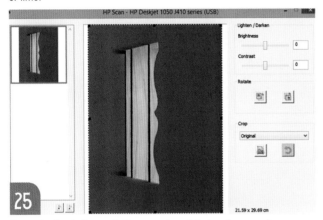

Place the front of your shelf compartment facing downward on your scanner so that you can scan the area to be burned in order to prepare the lettering. If you do not have a scanner, measure the height and width of the area in order to prepare a template in those dimensions on your computer.

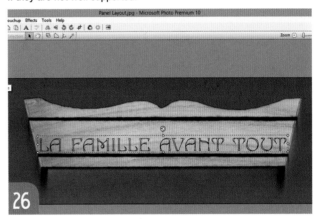

Select an appropriate font that matches the design and choose your text. I picked the French phrase for "family first" to adorn an item intended for display in the entrance to a family home. Adjust the size of the lettering to fit the area as fully as possible.

If necessary, stretch the height or width of the text until it fits the area between the tramlines as much as possible, ensuring the lettering is as visible as possible, as well as making the best use of the space available to you on the front panel.

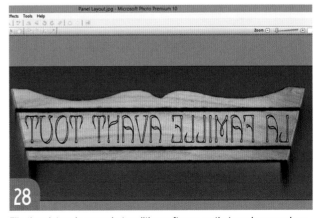

Flip the picture in your photo editing software so that you have a mirror image; this makes the tracing and transferring process much easier. Print it at the exact size you have specified so that the text is ready to be transferred onto the wood with no other adjustments necessary.

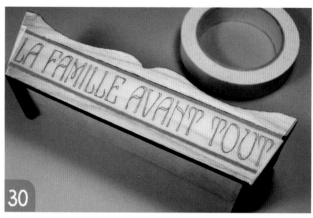

Cut a piece of tracing paper and trace the reversed lettering onto it in pencil. Using a freshly sharpened (or mechanical) pencil will ensure that your lines are as sharp and crisp as possible to maximize the quality of your transferred text, particularly if the font chosen is delicate.

Position the traced lettering carefully onto the shelf compartment with the drawn lettering facedown on the wooden surface. Secure the tracing paper in place with masking tape to make sure that it remains exactly in place once in position.

Transfer each word in turn onto the wood by scribbling on the rear of the tracing paper and removing the used sections immediately afterward. Burn each word in turn using a fine or bladed nib at a low-medium heat setting to give neat, precise lines with sharp points where needed.

Cut a few pieces of white cardstock paper to the required size necessary to fit inside each nameplate. Measure them accurately with a ruler to get the correct dimensions before cutting them out with either scissors or a scalpel. Use a pencil to write each name freehand in an italic style.

Use the point of a fine pyrography nib to burn each name into the white cardstock. You should not need anything over a medium heat setting to complete this. Add some decorative underlining if you wish. Thicken the vertical downstrokes of each letter to give the impression of calligraphy.

Use a hand drill to make small pilot holes for each screw needed to attach the antique brass hooks and nameplates. These holes should be considerably smaller than the maximum diameter of the screw thread in order to ensure a good secure fit. Do not fully drill through the entire plaque.

Attach each of the brass nameplates in the correct positions using their screws and an appropriately sized screwdriver. Once they are in place, complete the same process with the brass coat hooks, making sure they are secured as tightly as possible and flush with the plaque's surface.

Place each name card into one of the antique brass nameplates. If the size isn't completely right, you can trim any excess from the edges until they fit more comfortably. If they are far too small, you can always make another one to replace it.

Prepare the wooden shelf by adding a small amount of wood glue along each edge to be fixed to the plaque. Follow the instructions of the brand you're using for the best results; some glues recommend allowing it to sit for a few minutes before pressing the two items together, for example.

Place the plaque on a flat surface and press the wooden shelf down firmly onto it, keeping the pressure in place for a short while if needed. Make sure that you place the shelf in line with any marks that you have made to ensure that it is level and in the correct position for the design.

Use a cotton swab to neatly and cleanly remove any excess glue that is forced outward when the shelf is pressed into place. Running the cotton swab along the join can also assist in spreading the excess glue into the join for the best bond possible. Allow the item to dry well before use.

The Finished Results

Once the glue has fully dried, your wall organizer can be fixed to the wall of your choice. This type of wall décor can also be useful within the kitchen to keep the family's possessions in order. An item such as this can be tailored to suit the style of any household, so think about what suits the look of your home the best.

Dream Catcher Clock

Patterns on page 157

This idea developed as part of a pledge to make my wife a special clock of her very own as a gift. Originating from Native American culture, the dream catcher usually consists of a wrapped hoop with a woven web of string, with beads and feathers as decorative adornments, and is believed to act as a protective charm for the owner. I've always liked the story and imagery of the dream catcher and decided to create my own slant on this through pyrography. Using this idea to create a clock to hang on the wall also allowed me to think about different ways in which I could recreate the elements of the design.

The main ring and web formed the central elements on the clock face and are relatively simple to draw or create without the use of a complex pattern to copy. I used fine metal wire to mark out the numerals of the clock as I wanted to make something that delicately caught the eye when seen at certain angles. You could use thicker wire if you wanted to make the numbers more obviously visible, or possibly colored ribbon or cord as another alternative.

I had been thinking about ways to incorporate veneers into my pyrography designs for some time, and this project gave me the ideal opportunity. Commonly used in marquetry, the thinly sliced sheets are available in a variety of different woods, which allows you to readily introduce a range of shades, hues, and textures to your work. You can experiment with how these can be combined with your pyrography marks to see which work the best for your designs.

61

Equipment Needed:

- Pyrography machine of your choice and a selection of different pens/nibs
- Wooden clock kit (shaped blank and clock mechanism)
- Pencils, sharpener, and eraser—you can use a mechanical pencil if you prefer

- Ruler, compasses, protractor, tracing paper, scissors/scalpel, and pliers
- Cardstock
- Masking tape
- Hand drill and wood glue
- 6 flat disc beads

- Length of fine metal wire (ribbon or cord can be used as an alternative)
- Sheet of wood veneer
- Leather cord
- Selection of assorted small wooden beads

Mark out a border in pencil around the edge of the clock face; it should be approximately ⅜" (1cm) in size. Divide the clock face into equal quarters through the center with your ruler and use the protractor to create twelve segments for the hour markings.

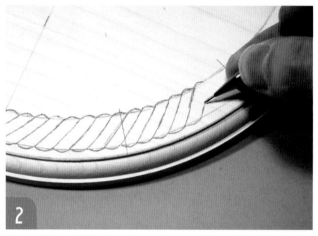

Draw a flattened "S" shape diagonally across the ⅜" (1cm) border in pencil and repeat the process all the way around to create a bound pattern effect. Each line does not have to be 100% identical, but you could always trace the line with tracing paper if you aren't confident drawing it freehand repeatedly.

Use a fine writing or bladed nib to burn over your lines and build up the pattern around the border. This should give the effect that the dream catcher is made up of a bound wooden hoop. Try to keep the lines as crisp and sharp as possible and avoid accidentally crossing them over.

Add another series of lines along the outside of the border and shade them in with the point of the nib. Use a medium to high temperature setting for a good contrast. This will give a bold definition to the border and make it stand out more from the background surface.

Add a series of lines for definition to each section in the border, by lightly drawing a fine nib away from the edge toward the center. This enhances the impression that the border is made up of something wrapped or bound by representing folds or creases in the "material" that you are drawing.

Use a shading nib such as a spoon point on a lower temperature to add some soft shading around the outlines you have burned. Flicking the nib and simultaneously lifting it away from the wood creates a graduated shade and ensures that you don't work the surface too heavily.

Cut out a shape from a piece of cardstock that resembles a teardrop in appearance. It should reach from the central hole to the edge of the border. Place it at the 12 o'clock position on the clock face and draw lightly around it in pencil.

Repeat the same process eleven more times, drawing around the teardrop-shaped template at each hour of the clock face to build up the woven spiderweb pattern that features in the center of all dream catchers.

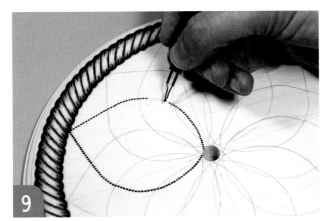

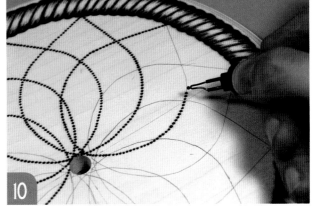

Use a writing or ballpoint nib on a medium-high temperature to neatly go along the first line of the web pattern, creating an even row of dots. Press lightly as you work and try to keep the marks as consistent as possible.

Work your way around every other teardrop line so that you build up the complete web pattern. Take care where lines cross so that you don't make any oversized marks. It is better to stop and restart on the other side rather than risk several dots joining together in an unsightly clump.

Dream Catcher Clock 63

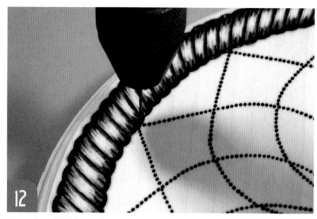

When all twelve of the teardrops have been burned, you should now have a delicate spiderweb within the center of your dream catcher. You can now erase any of the visible pencil lines that remain around the clock face at this point if you wish.

Use a fine drill bit, such as a ¹⁄₁₆" (1mm) or similar, to drill holes into the thicker border outlines to represent the Roman numerals at each hour on the clock face. Plan exactly how many holes you will need to create each numeral before you drill and mark them out in pencil for accuracy.

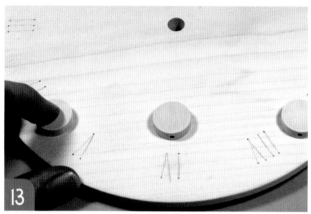

If it helps, you can add pencil lines between the holes on the rear of the clock to help you remember which numerals go where. (Remember that these will be a reversed mirror image of what you see on the front!) Attach three flat disc beads near the base of the clock on the rear with wood glue.

Cut small lengths of the metal wire and feed them through the fine holes to form your numerals. I chose very fine wire so that the numerals only catch the light at certain angles. You could use thicker wire if you wanted to make them more visible, or possibly ribbon or silk cord as an alternative.

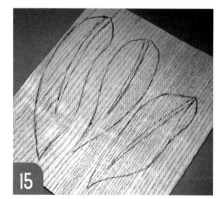

Draw out three basic feather shapes on your sheet of wooden veneer. Don't press down too hard with the pencil because the sheets of veneer are very fragile and will break easily if you work on them too heavily.

Build up the central stem of the feather by using a fine shading nib on a medium heat setting. The bowl of a spoon point nib is perfect for this purpose. Flick the nib away from the central line to fade the shading away toward the edge of the feather, with some longer lines for definition.

Use a bladed nib on a low temperature setting to create the outline of the feather, adding a few notches here and there for detail. Remember to work lightly at this stage so that you do not damage the veneer with the pressure of the blade.

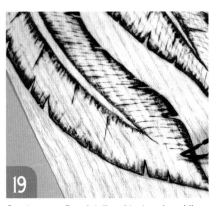

18 Add similar shading to the edges of the feather using your fine shading nib, similar to the shading that you have already added coming out from the center. Work in exactly the same manner as before but fade the shading back toward the center of the feather.

19 Create some fine detail and texture by adding some delicate lines with a bladed nib on a low temperature setting, working out diagonally at an angle from the center of the feather. If needed, use a real feather or a photo for reference to help you create the right effect.

20 Now for the fun part! Veneers are delicate by nature and can break if you try to cut them with a scalpel. Turn your bladed nib up to a higher temperature than usual and use it as a heated knife to carefully cut your feather out of the surrounding veneer sheet.

21 Once all three feathers are cut out of the veneer, gently glue the remaining three flat disc beads to the top of each on the rear and allow them to dry. Handle the veneer feathers delicately as they can easily break if treated roughly.

22 Cut three lengths of leather cord to a length of around 7⅞" to 9 ¹³⁄₁₆" (20 to 25cm) and tie a knot in the end of each. Thread them carefully through the flat disc bead attached to each of the feathers. Trim the end of the cord if necessary so that the knots are neat.

23 Decorate the assorted small wooden beads with a range of marks, textures, and patterns. The aim is just to create a quantity of beads that all look different and interesting when threaded together, so be as experimental as you wish with the effects that you create. Be sure not to burn your fingers!

24 Thread at least two to three beads down each of the three leather cords toward the feathers already attached to them. Make sure that you use a combination of beads that contrast with each other to vary the visual impact that they have.

Dream Catcher Clock **65**

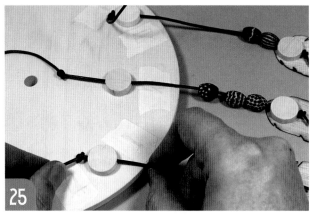

25 Thread the other end of the cord through the flat disc beads glued to the rear of the clock face and tie a knot to secure them in place; this will allow the feathers to hang below the clock. You can see that I have also added masking tape to the rear to protect the ends of the wire for the numerals.

26 Fit the clock mechanism through the central hole of the clock face and attach the hands, taking care not to damage the delicate feathers as you work. Insert a battery and your clock is now ready for display!

The Finished Results

You can now hang your dream catcher clock on the wall. If you wished, you could always add additional feathers or hanging beads. Feel free to take inspiration from dream catchers that you have seen elsewhere to get the exact look and feel that you are going for.

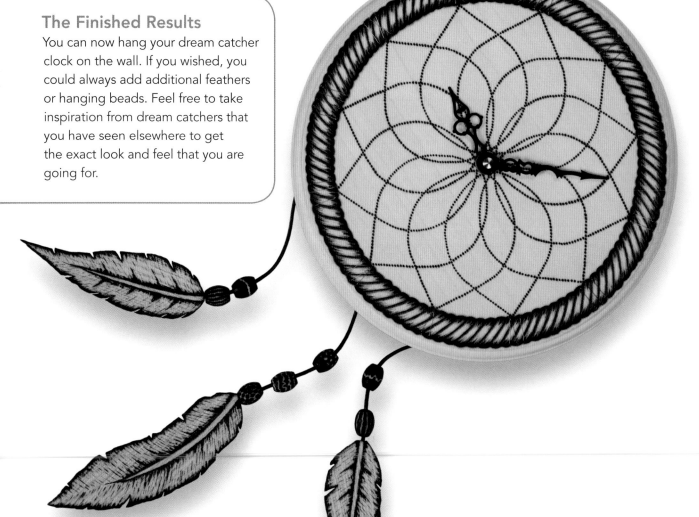

Stained Glass Wall Sconce

Patterns on pages 158–159

Many artists and craftspeople are inspired creatively by their surroundings, whether this is the place where they live or locations that they visit. This is also reflected in the number of potential customers that are keen to buy a memento that reminds them of a place that they enjoyed going to or living in. You can use this consideration when making pyrography designs that pay homage to a specific location or area. Incorporating place names, maps, landscape imagery, or identifiable landmarks into your designs is an exciting challenge that can bring you hours of pleasure.

One of my favorite locations in Wiltshire, the county in England where I was born and grew up, is the village of Avebury. This village is renowned internationally for its Neolithic stone circle, the largest in the world. Stonehenge may be the more instantly recognizable landmark for many tourists, but Avebury's stone circle and henge (the bank and ditch around the stones) is over 1,000 years older than its local relation, is much larger in scale, and is extremely impressive in its own right. With a diameter of over 1,000 ft. (305m), the monument is so large that it surrounds much of the village and is divided into four quarters by the main road running through it. Visitors can walk freely among the standing stones and really take in the atmosphere and spirituality of the prehistoric site. The site is particularly popular at key points of the year, including the Summer and Winter Solstices, when druids and other followers of ancient beliefs celebrate the changing of the seasons.

To reflect the mystical nature of the megalithic monument, I decided to design and decorate a wooden candle sconce in the style of a stained glass window, incorporating associated pagan elements into the composition to reflect the many that worship the earliest religions amidst the stone circle. I also selected a photograph of some standing stones (taken by local wildlife and landscape photographer,

Angela Norman) in order to add a visual image of the physical landscape into my design. You could apply the same principles of this project to many other items, such as decorative plaques or pairs of bookends.

Equipment Needed:

- Pyrography machine of your choice and a selection of different pens/nibs
- Wooden candle wall sconce (with protective metal candle holder)
- Computer, printer, and paper
- Pencils, sharpener, and eraser—you can use a mechanical pencil if you prefer
- Ruler, protractor, circle template, and compasses
- Tracing paper, masking tape, and scissors
- Screwdriver

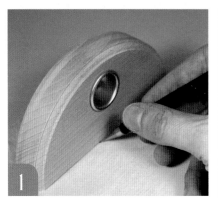

1 Mark the position of the candle sconce's shelf lightly by running a pencil around it before using a screwdriver to dismantle the wooden blank. This will make the item easier to work on by separating it into two halves, since it can be difficult working down into the right angle where both parts meet.

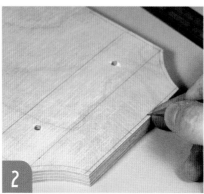

2 Draw a running border approximately ⅛" (3mm) from the edges of the main body of the blank. Use your finger as a running guide around the plaque to make an even line that is the same distance from the edge all the way around, holding your hand and pencil in a fixed manner for accuracy.

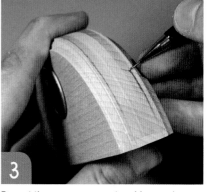

3 Repeat the same process to add a running border around the main curved edge of the sconce's shelf section. Make every effort to ensure that the width and spacing of the border is exactly the same as that around the main body of the blank for consistency.

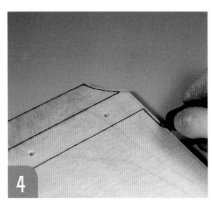

4 Use a fine or bladed nib to neatly burn the outline that you have created around the edge of the main body. A medium heat temperature setting should be just right. Ensure that the line is as even and fluid as possible with no inconsistencies where separate sections join when moving your hand.

5 Repeat the same process to burn the borderline onto the curved surface edge of the shelf. Working on curved surfaces can be tricky, so make sure that you are comfortable as you burn. Ensure a good grip of the wooden blank when you get to the ends so that you do not slip or make a mistake.

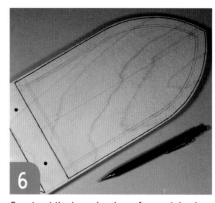

6 Construct the inner borders of your stained glass window panel using a ruler and pencil. Try to make your design as precise and symmetrical as you can at this stage of the preparation. It will help to guarantee a positive result when you start burning the design into the wood.

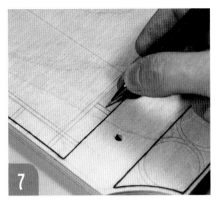

7

Add detail to the design lightly in pencil using your ruler and circle templates. Use the central halfway line to ensure your design is balanced evenly. If you start to break the borders up into smaller "panes," try to keep these as equal in size as possible so that the design looks balanced.

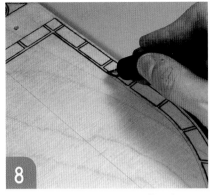

8

Use a fine or bladed nib on a medium heat setting to burn in the detail of the panel that you have just drawn. Regularly burning the marks that you have made, rather than drawing everything in one go and burning it the same way, ensures that you do not lose any of your design while lightly drawn.

9

Constructing a Celtic cross as the centerpiece of your design can be achieved easily from scratch. Draw the basic cross structure using five squares in a vertical line, adding two squares on either side of the second one down for the crosspiece. Arrange these squares evenly around the centerline.

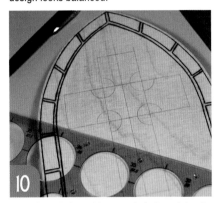

10

Draw four circles with your circle template at the point where the crosspiece intersects the main vertical line of five squares. Draw lightly with your pencil so that the lines can be easily erased when no longer required.

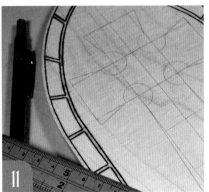

11

Use a ruler to extend the top, side, and bottom edges of the cross in pencil. As an example, I extended each section line by 3/16" (5mm) on both sides. Use a ruler to join the extended ends to the circles you drew at the last stage, giving a diagonal slant to each new edge of the Celtic cross.

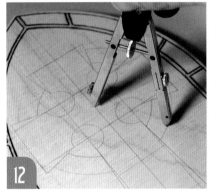

12

Use a pair of compasses to draw two concentric circles, using the middle of the central square as the center point. Draw only the sections of the two circles that are visible behind the cross in order to give a 3D impression to the design. The circular band will then appear to sit under the main cross.

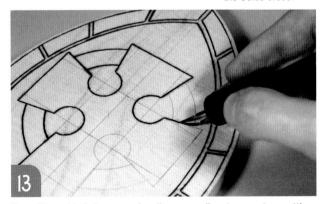

13

Use a fine or bladed pyrography nib on a medium temperature setting to draw the outlines of the cross design in the same way that you have completed all outlines included in the design so far. Pay attention to any areas where the pencil lines meet or intersect so that you do not make an error.

14

Add parallel pencil lines approximately 1/8" (3mm) away from the lines that you have burned for the cross so far in order to create an identical visual impression to the rest of the border. This will enable you to shade the lines of the cross so that the thickness matches those surrounding it exactly.

Stained Glass Wall Sconce   69

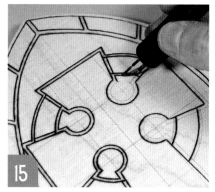

Burn these additional outlines around each section of the cross so that it is surrounded by a pair of parallel outlines on every side. You will be shading within these lines in due course, so it does not matter if they cross unnecessarily as long as the main body of the cross and circle are clear.

Work your way around the surface of the design with an eraser in order to get rid of any unwanted pencil lines that you have used to create the structure of the design. A soft eraser should have no issue removing lines that have been lightly drawn, so remember never to press hard on the wood!

Use a small shading nib, such as a spoon point, to start shading the border outlines. Set the machine at a medium-high temperature in order to create a solid, dark tone. Make sure that you shade past the lines drawn in step 1 so that no plain wood is visible at the join when the shelf is reattached.

Continue the shading with care around the entire outline border, including the cross itself. Make sure that you do not shade outside of your crisp outlines. Instead, use just the very tip of the nib if necessary so that you do not have too much heated metal in contact with the wooden surface, and take your time.

Use a shading nib to fill in the borderlines on the shelf of the sconce as well. Remember to position the blank carefully as you work and support it firmly as you work so that you do not slip. A burned finger is not a pleasant experience, and neither is making a mistake in a precise design!

Start to add more detail to your design lightly in pencil. Add 3D structure to the body of your cross and draw in some other decorative elements, such as a pentagram and the start of a triple-moon design at the bottom. Trace sections from your chosen landscape photograph to add local interest.

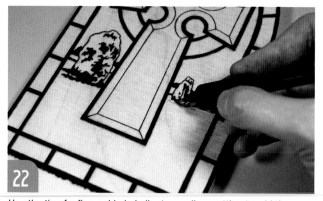

Use a fine or bladed nib at a low-medium heat setting to start adding the lines of definition to the cross. Keep these lines as straight and sharp as possible, while also taking great care to ensure that they join neatly at any angles or corners. The 3D effect is now starting to be established.

Use the tip of a fine or bladed nib at a medium setting to add the decorative detail of the landscape image. Make sure the marks are bold and dark for maximum contrast, keeping the image as a monotone representation of the landmarks you have chosen, rather than using delicate graduated shading.

23 After shading any other design elements you've added (such as my pentagram circle), draw fine lines with a bladed nib that radiate from a central point to add visual interest to any sections of sky in the image. These lines add interest to the composition and work well with the thicker border outlines.

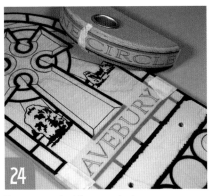

24 Prepare any text for your design on your computer, adjusting the dimensions so that it fills any areas to the exact size you require. Trace the letters with a pencil onto tracing paper and stick them in place on the wooden blanks with masking tape so that they do not move during the transfer process.

25 After scribbling on the tracing paper to transfer the letters onto the wood, use a fine or bladed nib at a medium temperature setting, and carefully burn each letter into the surface. Keep the lines sharp and tight, particularly any fine points or serifs, so that the lettering looks immaculate.

26 Continue the same process with the bladed nib at the same heat setting in order to burn the text onto the edge of the sconce shelf. As with the previous stages of the project, be especially careful as you work on the curved edge so that you do not go outside of the pencil marks in any way.

27 Add some bold stippled shading with the point of a fine or bladed nib to give contrast to the design where needed. A spear point at a medium temperature setting is my "weapon of choice" for dotted marks such as these. Spread the dots further apart and with less frequency for a lighter tone.

28 Add any more detail around the main design as necessary. I added a few irregular horizontal lines to represent the grass around the base of the stones, spreading these further apart as I moved down in order to visually represent depth with the foreground being "closer" to the eye of the viewer.

29

Explore any other areas where you can add more decorative features to your design. I added a rope pattern to the circular band behind the cross, drawing a series of repeated "S" shapes across two pencil lines and then burning over them with a fine or bladed nib to make them permanent.

Add areas of bold stippled shading around and behind the rope pattern that you have created in the same way that you applied it in step 27. This helps to give a sense of depth by lifting the rope away from its background, as well as differentiating it from other sections of the whole design.

Use a fine or bladed nib at a low temperature setting to add a series of small marks with a quick flicking motion, working away from each of the radiating sky lines in turn at a 90° angle. This adds another form of subtle visual contrast to the various elements of the design.

Time to add some definition to the main cross of the design. Imagine a light source shining down from a specific point above the cross. Which sides would be illuminated? Which would be in shadow? Use a small shading nib to add dark stippled dots to the edges that would not be in the light.

Now apply the same principle to the curved edges at the center of the cross, picturing where the light would fall and where the shadows would be. Add stippled shading to the main areas of shadow but fade these outward from each area in order to represent the light across the curved surfaces.

Add a series of parallel lines down the sides of the cross that you feel would receive the most light from your imaginary source of illumination. Use a bladed nib at a low heat setting and reduce the frequency of the lines as you move down each edge to add contrast and depth to the image.

35

Apply some more textural details to the scenery and landscape images behind your cross. Additional dots on the standing stones give an impression of their rough texture, while rows of fine vertical marks behind them help to signify the fence line in the distance of the background.

36

Add some sharp lines in the corners of the remaining plain border panels. Work around the whole design, adding "L" or "V" shapes in opposing corners of each separate panel to give definition to them. A bladed nib at a low heat setting is ideal; drag and flick the nib off the surface quickly as you work.

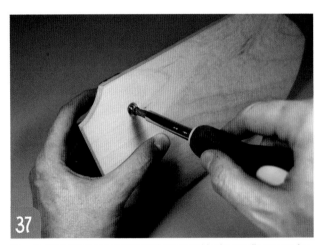

37

Now that the burning is completed, reassemble the candle sconce by attaching the shelf back to its original position, using a screwdriver to tighten the screws as much as possible. This is important so that the shelf is secure and level before anything is placed on it.

The Finished Results

Your beautiful sconce is now ready for display on a wall. If you wanted to develop an even more vibrant design, you could always consider applying colored inks or paints to such an item for a vibrant and realistic stained glass effect. One point to remember . . . never leave a burning candle unattended. Also, only ever use wooden blanks that have a protective metal or glass holder for the candle itself, and do not leave them lit for prolonged periods of time.

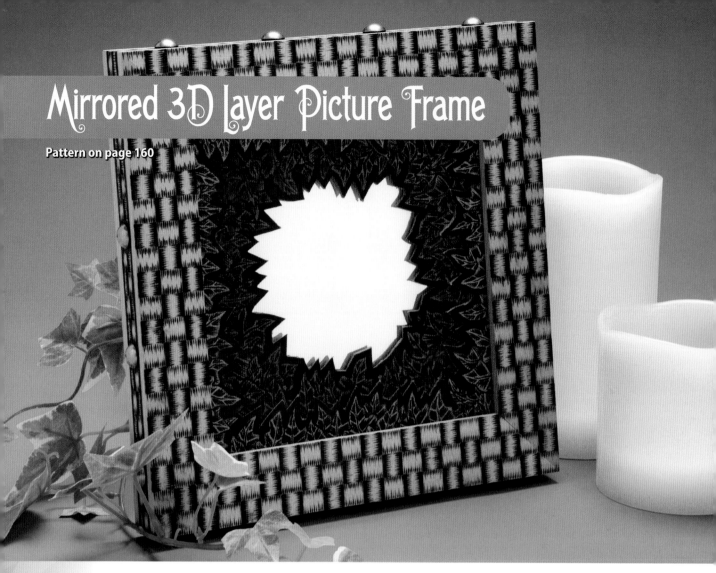

Mirrored 3D Layer Picture Frame

Pattern on page 160

Picture frames are one of my favorite items to work with when using pyrography. I regularly work on larger frames for customers to make personalized commission pieces, so it is a real pleasure to sometimes bring the scale down and create something smaller as a new challenge. Creating a piece that is designed purely to be beautiful and decorative is a true challenge. Adding a mirror to the frame accentuates this because the frame is displaying an item that invites the viewer to look into it for a prolonged period of time. If there are flaws or faults in the design you create around a mirror, the chances of someone noticing them are massively increased!

The focus behind this project was to combine my love of texture and pattern with a sense of depth. I have only worked with leather as a surface for

pyrography on a small handful of occasions, and therefore several sheets of vegetable-tanned leather have sat in my stock of supplies for some time, just waiting for the opportunity to be used. I decided to use the leather to make decorative mounts that sit inside the frame above a mirror so that a sense of depth is created when you gaze into it. I also utilized the different natural tones of the leather to enhance this feeling, using a darker sheet underneath a paler leather to subtly differentiate between the two.

If you prefer, this design could be developed to hold a photograph rather than a mirror; the choice is completely yours. As with many of the other projects in this book, you can also apply the same principles that are featured here to create your own bespoke design with a completely different theme than the one I have used.

Equipment Needed:

- Pyrography machine of your choice and a selection of different pens/nibs
- Square wooden frame
- Sheet(s) of vegetable tanned leather
- Piece of mirror glass (to fit inside the frame)
- Pencils, sharpener, and eraser—you can use a mechanical pencil if you prefer
- Ruler and circle template
- Cutting board/mat and scissors/scalpel
- Hand drill and center punch
- Quantity of copper upholstery pins

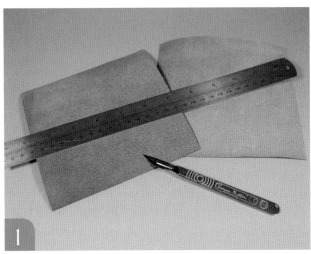

Cut two pieces of vegetable-tanned leather to size using a scalpel and cutting mat. These should be cut so that they fit snugly within your chosen frame. If you can, select two sections of the available leather sheets that are different in shade or color, as this will add contrast to your design.

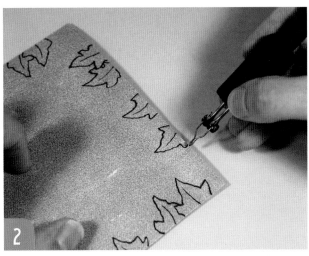

Start to build up a border around the edge of the first piece of leather, drawing a series of leaves by hand with a spear nib (or a similar type of nib). I have used ivy leaves for this project due to their distinctive shape, but you can use any leaf that you choose. Oak leaves are another popular option.

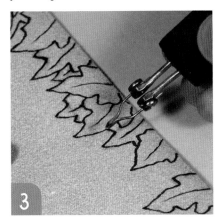

Continue to work around the edge of the leather to build up a solid pattern of leaves. Add some leaves in the background behind others to increase the sense of depth in the design. Try to make sure that the lines are as bold and consistent as possible for the best contrast.

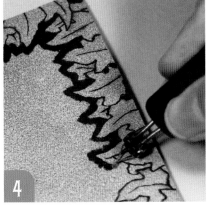

Once you have finished drawing the border, add a dark border of shading around the inside edge of the pattern using a shading nib, such as a small spoon point. This should create a dark shaded area at least ⅛" to ³⁄₁₆" (3 to 4mm) or so from the leaves in readiness for the inner window aperture being cut out.

Use a fine or bladed nib on a low-medium temperature to start adding some detail to the body of the leaves. Work around each leaf in turn to give the shapes more definition. Using lines instead of shading increases the boldness and definition of your work, particularly at such a small scale.

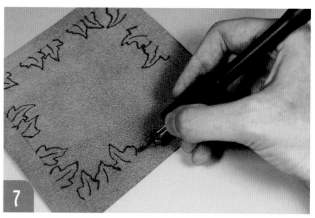

Prepare your second piece of leather by drawing a border in pencil along each edge. This represents the area that will not be visible when this piece is placed below the first layer you have made. Measure the first piece's decoration to work out how much space needs to be left at the edge.

Start to draw another border of leaves on the second leather layer, but work from the borderlines that you have drawn on this piece, rather than at the edge of the material itself. This will guarantee that the design on this layer will be visible when the other piece is placed on top in the frame.

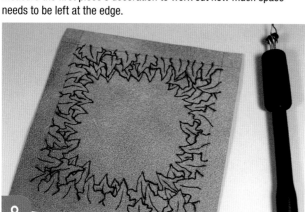

Complete the border on the second layer in the same manner as you did for the first leather layer. Remember to avoid leaving any gaps in the design by adding leaves behind the first ones you draw so that the design is substantial when it is cut out.

Shade the background of the leaves on this second layer in an identical way to the method used for the first leather layer. Use a small spoon point nib at a medium temperature setting to get a consistent dark shaded burn across the surface of the leather.

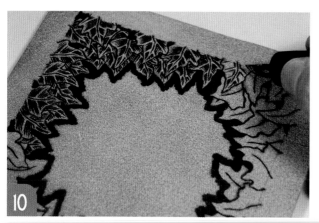

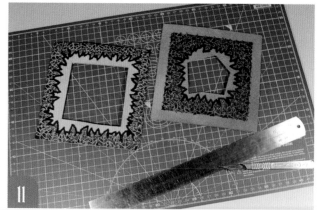

Repeat the process for adding detail and definition to the leaves themselves (with a fine or bladed nib at a low temperature setting) as you did for the first leather layer. This should be possible freehand and should not require any drawing or preparation first; just trust your hand and eye!

It is now time to cut the window apertures from each piece of leather. Use a sharp scalpel and work on a cutting mat. Cut out a rough shape of waste material from the middle of each piece initially before you start the detailed shaping that forms the decorative border itself.

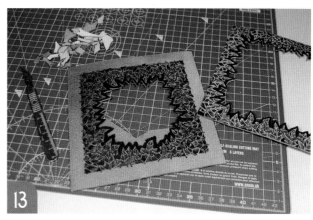

Use light and repeated scalpel strokes to cut through the tough leather sheets, rather than rushing and pressing hard. Gently work away from each leaf to create the shaped window aperture, removing each small offcut as you go. Take your time and be careful not to slip with the scalpel.

Once you have completely cut out the border of the first leather layer, move onto the second piece and repeat the process. You should now be able to see how the first layer will successfully fit over the second layer to display the individual patterns contained on each.

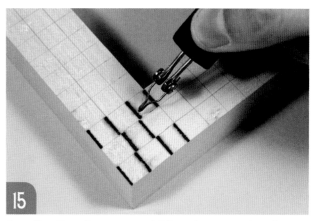

Prepare the layout on your square frame by dividing each side into three with two pencil lines, measuring the sizes carefully and drawing them out with a ruler. When repeated on every side, this should create a grid of squares that will be used to create your decorative textured pattern.

Use a fine nib, such as a spear point, to work your way down the inside edges of alternate squares on the grid that you have drawn on the frame. Our intention is to build up a surface pattern that will resemble woven material by using only simple shading and directional mark making.

Work down one edge of the alternate squares, dragging and flicking the point of the fine nib toward the middle of the square in neat rows to create a textured pattern. Repeat this identically in the other squares that you have started to add shading to.

Turn the frame around and repeat the same process on the opposite side of the squares you have just shaded. You should now be able to see how the pattern is going to look when this technique is used around the whole frame.

Mirrored 3D Layer Picture Frame   77

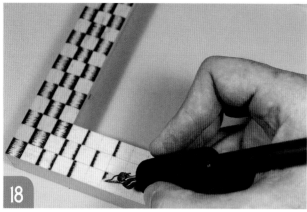

18

Continue the same routine around every other alternate square to fill the whole frame with identically textured blocks. Take great care not to ruin the pattern by accidentally shading two adjoining squares by mistake. Making an error like this can be extremely frustrating!

19

Once the first squares are all completed, we are now going to create the same effect but while working at a 90° angle to the directional lines on the initial textural work. Turn the frame around and use a fine bladed nib to flick away from the edge of the remaining squares toward the middle area.

20

Turn the frame around 180° and repeat the same marks with the bladed nib on the opposite side of the squares you are now working on. You should be able to see how the texture is building up to suggest strips of material being woven over and under each other in sequence.

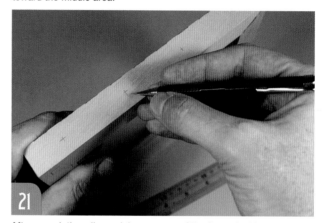

21

After completing all remaining squares of the frame in this way, measure the midpoint along every side of the frame and mark out four or five points at regular distances to show where the copper upholstery pins will be added as decoration.

22

Carefully drill each point indicated with a ¹⁄₁₆" (1mm) drill bit to act as a pilot hole for the upholstery pins. Hold or secure the frame carefully while drilling in this way as the delicate drill bits can be easily snapped if the frame moves at any point during the process.

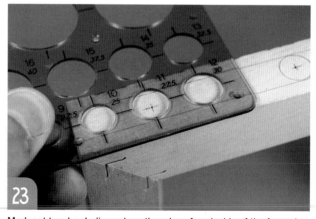

23

Mark out two borderlines along the edge of each side of the frame in pencil with a ruler. Use a circle template to draw a circle around each drilled hole as centrally as possible. The circle you draw should be larger than the head of the upholstery pin in order to create a shadow effect when shaded.

Shade the area within each borderline on every side of the frame, and fully shade the circular areas around each hole. Use a small spoon point nib (or similar) at a medium-high temperature setting for maximum contrast and definition. Leave a small, unburned area around the hole itself for visibility.

Draw out a partial grid pattern lightly in pencil within the border that you have created, using the same dimensions as the squares on the top face of the frame. The intention here is to make it look as if the same pattern is continuing across the sides of the frame as well.

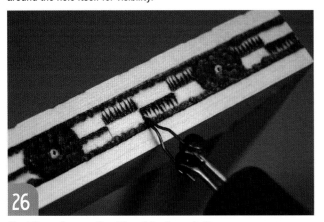

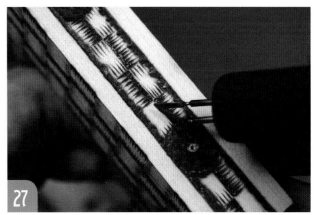

Start the pattern on the sides of the frame in the same way as you did on the main face in step 15: working on alternate squares with a spear point nib, and using marks in a consistent direction to build up the first impressions of the same texture.

Swap over to a fine bladed nib and repeat the process by adding the fine lines in the remaining squares at a 90° angle to those that you have just burned, flicking the point of the nib gently toward the middle of the squares and lifting away so that the lines fade out naturally.

Firmly press the copper upholstery pins into the pilot holes that you drilled earlier, gradually working your way around the whole frame until all are successfully inserted. If necessary, place the frame on a soft surface and gently tap the upholstery pins with a hammer to ensure they go in completely.

You can now assemble the whole item, adding the two leather layers on top of the mirror glass before securing them within the frame. If you wish, you can leave the glass of the frame inside to provide protection for the leather and mirror, or you can remove it so that they are free to be touched.

The Finished Results

This project is ideally suited to creating small, beautiful picture or mirror frames, but there is also nothing at all to prevent you from "scaling up" and applying the same process to larger frames. If you struggle to find larger pieces of leather, you could always consider working on cardboard mounts; these are able to withstand pyrography application and are also a lot easier to cut and shape.

Zodiac Solitaire Game Board

Patterns on page 161

Making your own games can be a fantastic, rewarding experience. Solitaire is the perfect example of this since a beautiful playing board with carefully selected pieces can also make a great centerpiece for a table or sideboard. You can tailor the theme or style of the design in countless ways to suit the person it is intended for, as well as choosing the marbles, beads, or pegs to accompany it. You could even make your own playing pieces from wooden beads, burning patterns or textures into the surface. The box used to elevate the playing surface also allows for the storage of the playing pieces when not in use, as well as concealing a secret "mystery touch" described below.

For this project, I have used a theme derived from the astrological signs of the zodiac, working in a bold manner with my pyrography to ensure a high level of contrast. As well as decorating the game board's border and the base of the piece with the

symbols and constellations for each individual star sign, I decided to experiment with the use of light in my design to give a playful technological slant to the whole item. I have used an LED lighting unit (often used in swimming pools or garden ponds) to enable colored lights to vividly illuminate the game board from below and within. The lighting unit that I chose has a remote control in order to select between a range of different colors and interval settings so that the game itself becomes alive at the touch of a button.

The craggy, translucent marbles that I selected look like small meteors to continue the theme, and complement the effects of the flashing colored lights. The overall effect in combination looks especially stunning when activated in low light conditions, resulting in a design that is also a real talking point.

Equipment Needed:

- Pyrography machine of your choice and a selection of different pens/nibs
- 9¹³⁄₁₆" (25cm) round solid wooden plaque/blank (or similar)
- Pencil, sharpener, ruler, eraser, pair of compasses, and protractor
- Circle stencil/template
- Tracing paper and scissors
- Center punch, hammer, and a small screwdriver
- Hand drill or similar
- 32 decorative marbles for the playing pieces
- Blank wooden box with a hinged lid that is attached by screws (IMPORTANT: the box at its widest must not be bigger than the diameter of the round wooden blank)
- Electronic LED light unit (preferably with a range of colors and flash interval settings, plus its own remote control)

Start by measuring and marking the center point of the round plaque blank using a ruler and pencil. You will then need to draw horizontal and vertical lines running through the center point at right angles to each other.

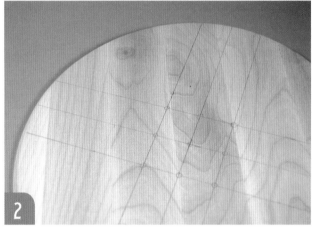

Mark out two more equidistant lines on either side of the lines running through the center point. This should form a cross of three parallel lines. Circle the points where the lines intersect in the middle, as these will form the central holes for the playing pieces.

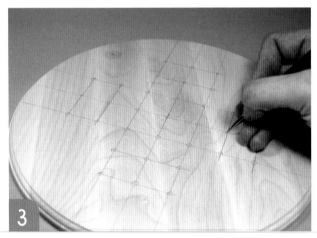

Measure out two more lines the same distance apart along each arm of the cross that you have drawn. Circle the six points on each of the four arms where the lines intersect. You should now have marked a total of 33 points where the lines intersect.

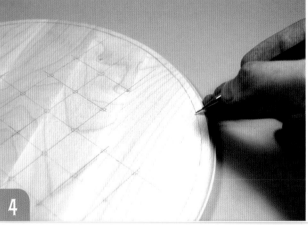

Draw a border approximately ³⁄₁₆" (5mm) in from the edge of the plaque. You can measure and draw it with a pair of compasses from the center point. Alternatively, run your fingers around the edge while holding the pencil in a fixed grip at the required spacing to get a basic border marked out.

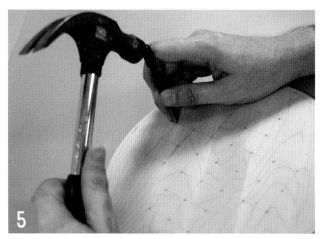

Mark each of the 33 playing holes by using a center punch and tapping it with a hammer. This does not need to be done with substantial effort. You are simply aiming to create a small indentation to assist when drilling.

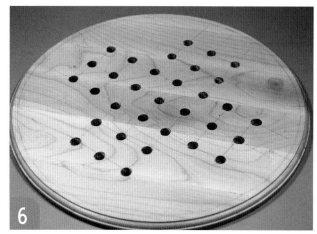

Drill each of the holes to create the playing area. A hand drill is perfectly adequate if you do not have access to a drill press (pillar drill) or similar. Don't worry too much if the holes are slightly off center when working by hand, as the overall finish will not be affected once the pyrography decoration is added.

Use the circle template to start drawing circles around each of the holes you have drilled. These should be around ⅛" to ³⁄₁₆" (3 to 4mm) bigger than the size of the holes themselves. The circles should also be offset slightly so that they almost touch the edge of the drilled hole at one point.

Use the bowl of a spoon point nib to fill in the circles that you have marked out around the edges of the drilled holes. This is the first step in building up an irregular pattern of circles. You can see that each circle is positioned at a slightly different offset rather than all being centered around the holes.

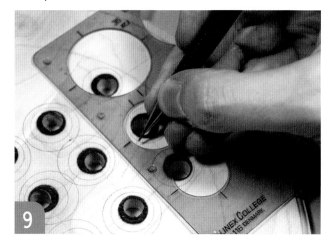

Draw two more circles around each hole, each approximately ³⁄₁₆" (4 to 5mm) bigger than the previous one. These should, again, be offset at different positions (rather than centered), and can also overlap in places with rings around the surrounding holes as the pattern expands. Add another pencil line parallel to the circumference of the outer edge so that you have a border surrounding the playing area.

Use the spoon point nib at a medium heat setting again to fill in and shade the next ring that you have created. Join the rings together where they cross and intersect with those around them. Do not shade across the pencil line of the outer border; keep that ring free of shading where lines meet.

Once the shading of those circles is complete, repeat the process again by drawing another larger circle around each of the drilled holes. You will now be joining the pattern together rather than creating distinct rings due to the holes being positioned close together.

Drill a series of smaller holes (around ¹⁄₁₆" to ⅛" [2 to 3mm]) at random intervals around the inner playing space area. These should only be a few millimeters deep and not go through the whole plaque. They are merely decorative and intended to add some other detail and definition to the playing area.

Shade the areas between the outer border and the most recent circles with a shading nib. A spoon nib can be handy for working its way into acute angles as you work. Stay out of the surrounding border and take care not to shade into the small, decorative partial holes that you drilled in the previous step.

Use a broad shading nib at a medium-high temperature to shade around the edge of the plaque and fill in the ³⁄₁₆" (5mm) border that you created. This should form a crisp and bold outline to the plaque, and will also leave a plain ring free from any burning so far for the decorative border.

Mark out the spacing for the decorative border in pencil. Divide the border into twelve equal segments, using a protractor if needed. Aim to work approximately 1/16" (2mm) inside of the areas previously burned and leave a gap of the same distance between each segment.

Draw out your symbols to represent the signs of the zodiac in each of the twelve segments, taking care to ensure that you place them in the correct order as you work your way around the border. Place them as centrally as possible within each segment, making sure they all face the same direction.

Use a spoon point shading nib to mark out the zodiac signs by shading around the outside of them. Shade inside the outer lines of each segment as well to start building up the decorative border. Work to an approximate distance of shading no more than 1/8" (3mm) from the lines that you have drawn.

Turn the pyrography machine down to a low temperature setting and start to shade around each zodiac sign with a soft stippling pattern. Make sure you're dotting the nib softly against the surface and filling each segment with a delicately shaded texture.

Turn the pyrography machine up a little higher and work back over the shading in each segment again with another layer of similar stippling. This will gradually build up a textured feel to the shading with marks of different intensity, so take your time as you shade.

Turn the pyrography machine up a third time and repeat the process again; it should now be on a medium to high setting. Use your stippled shading more intensely near the segment edges and the lettering—with fewer dots in the center of each area—for a richer sense of graduated texture.

20

Shade around the lip of the round plaque to create another decorative band; this will add definition when the playing area is attached to the base in the next stages. Use a broad shading nib on a medium-high setting, working the shading as evenly as possible for a consistent finish.

21

Dismantle your chosen wooden box so that it can be used to make the base of the playing board. Keep the screws and hinges safely to one side. You will not need the lid of the box, so it can be recycled for another purpose or project.

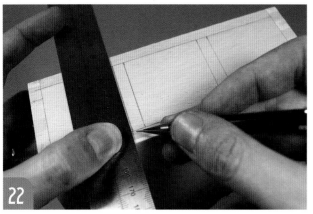

22

Mark out three equally sized panels on each side of the box using a ruler and pencil. You should then have a total of twelve squares or rectangles across all four faces, and each will correspond to a different constellation for each sign of the zodiac.

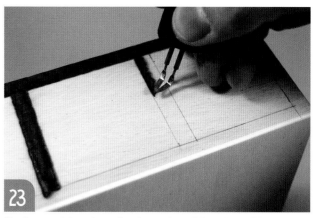

23

Shade around the edges of each panel on all four sides of the box so that you have a distinct dark border to work within. Use whichever shading nib you prefer. If you find it easier, you could burn all of the lines with a bladed nib first to ensure that they are as straight and sharp as possible.

24

Trace and transfer each of your constellations into their corresponding panels. Be sure that they are all placed in the correct order so they line up with the correct zodiac symbol on the playing board when fixed together. A bladed or spear nib is best for the detail of the constellation and accompanying text.

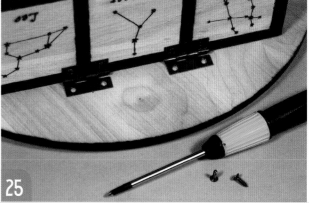

25

Position the base of the box so that it is correctly aligned with the design on the playing board and use the hinges of the box to attach the two parts together. Once this is done, you can place your electronic LED light unit inside the box and position your playing pieces on top, ready for action.

The Finished Results

Once the marbles have been put into position, they should be illuminated by the LED light unit below. This creates an amazing effect when the game is played in the dark. It's played similarly to chess; you skip marbles over one another until a single marble remains. Beautiful by day and stunning by night, this decorative game will look fantastic on display in your home.

Dragon Table Catchall Bowl

Pattern on page 162

It is my genuine belief that most people in the world have somewhere that they stash all their little random "bits 'n' bobs." It might be a drawer, a mug, a box, or something else, but I think we all have some place that we put those small items we simply don't want to lose, even if we are not sure when we will need them next! These items could include loose change, screws, earring backs, rings, safety pins, keys, or many more similar items. Ultimately, we all have somewhere that is our first resort when we need to put something in a safe location where it will not then go missing when we next need it.

If we are going to have such a place, why not design something specific to make it more beautiful and less random? I bought a small turned wooden bowl online with a view to designing a "catchall bowl." It could be used on a workbench, on a bedside table, or in a kitchen display cabinet, but the intention is still the same irrespective of where it is placed: to make something that is not just useful but also decorative and a pleasure to look at.

I also took advantage of the curved surface of the blank bowl to try out some new iridescent paints that I had recently received. Due to their glittering qualities, these paints change in hue when viewed from different angles and give a beautiful decorative finish, particularly across shaped or irregular surfaces. The shape and form of the bowl reminded me of half of an egg, so I decided to feed my lifelong fascination with dragons and create a design based on that love of the awe-inspiring mythical beasts. The dragon's infamous obsession with treasure hoards gave me an idea for a small surprise within the bowl as well.

Equipment Needed:

- Pyrography machine of your choice and a selection of different pens/nibs
- Small wooden bowl/dish
- Pencils, sharpener, and eraser—you can use a mechanical pencil if you prefer
- Cardstock, cutting mat, and scissors/scalpel
- Tracing paper, masking tape, and superglue
- Selection of iridescent wood paints/stains
- Paintbrush, palette, and scrap wood (for testing the paints)
- Decorative crystal, gem, or marble

Add an irregular, dark shaded edge along the bottom of the bowl, working out from the flat surface that the item stands on. A spoon point nib is perfect for adding this area of shadow; use a medium-high temperature setting.

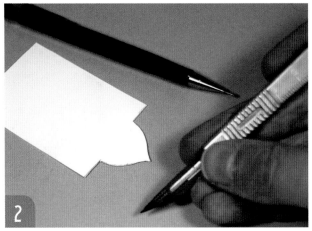

Draw out the shape of a scale in pencil on a piece of cardstock before cutting it out carefully with a scalpel or pair of scissors. This will then be used as a template for the outer surface of the bowl in order to quickly reproduce identical shapes (rather than trying to draw the whole design freehand).

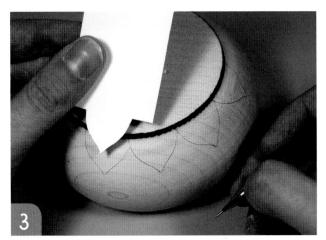

Start at the bottom edge of the bowl and draw around the scale stencil you have made with a pencil. Move the stencil around slightly, overlapping the line you previously drew, and add another scale. Work your way all around the edge until you have joined up into a whole row of scales.

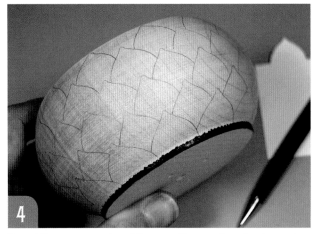

Repeat the process again, adding row after row of overlapping scales as you work your way toward the top edge of the bowl. Stagger the lines so that each scale neatly fits between two previous ones. Look at pictures showing the scales of a snake or lizard for guidance if you need to.

5 Use a fine or bladed nib at a low temperature setting to burn the outline of each individual scale in turn. Start at the bottom of the bowl as you did when drawing them.

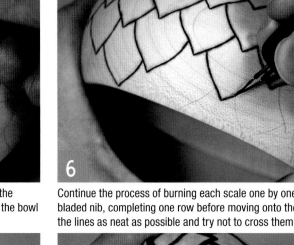

6 Continue the process of burning each scale one by one with the bladed nib, completing one row before moving onto the next. Keep the lines as neat as possible and try not to cross them over in error.

7 Change to a fine shading nib, such as a small spoon point nib, and select a medium-high heat setting. Add a small shaded border along the outside of each scale to give the impression that the overlapping scales create a shadow.

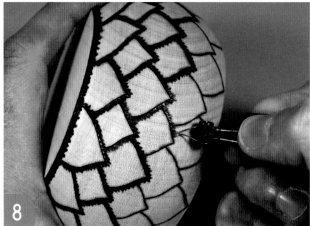

8 Continue shading around the outside of each individual scale as you work your way around each row before moving onto the next one. The shadow effect helps to give more depth and substance to the pattern, rather than leaving it merely as a flat graphic representation.

9 Use a broad shading nib on a high temperature setting to fill in the areas with no scales at the top of the bowl. This also helps to create the impression that the dragon egg has cracked open for the creature within to hatch!

10 Shaped pyrography nibs can be useful for stamping or branding their imprint into the wood. I used this broad V-shaped shading nib to create a ridge in the middle of each scale. The temperature needs to be high for the nib's large surface area to create a solid, dark impression in the wood.

Add linear detail to one half of every scale by using a fine or bladed nib on a medium heat setting. Use a row of lines that all radiate into the center of the scale on one side so that a sense of texture is created.

Add an area of contrasting stippled texture to the opposite side of each scale for contrast. A fine nib, such as a spear point, is perfect for creating this dotted pattern. These nibs do not require a substantially high temperature setting to create well-defined marks in the wooden surface.

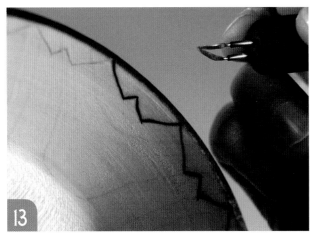

Use the fine or bladed nib to add a row of scales inside the bowl that echoes the shapes on the outside. You can either use the scale template or draw it freehand if you prefer. This will help to enhance the visual impression of a cracked egg when viewed from many angles.

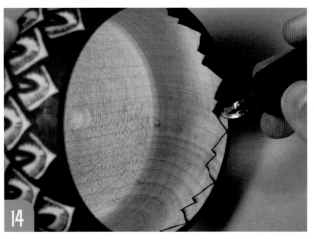

Fill in the inner row of scales by blocking them in with a broad shading nib. Be careful when working to ensure that you do not go over and ruin the crisp scales outline that you have drawn. Hold the bowl carefully in a firm grip while working on the inner surface.

Print the dragon pattern at the correct size to best fit into the base of the bowl. The aim is for the baby dragon to look like it is curled up and napping as a surprise to the beholder. Draw it onto the tracing paper and cut it to shape, ready for the transfer process to begin.

Turn the tracing paper over so that the drawn dragon outline is in contact with the base of the bowl and secure it firmly in place with pieces of masking tape. The central claw of the dragon should be placed in the middle of the bowl (the reason for this will become clear later).

Scribble on the tracing paper so that the dragon design is successfully transferred onto the wood. Press firmly to ensure that the design is visible when the tracing paper is removed, but not too hard if your bowl is made of a softer wood that is at risk of becoming dented by pencil impressions on the surface.

Use a fine or bladed nib on a low temperature setting to draw the outline of the baby dragon. Take your time if the position of your hand is slightly awkward due to the depth of the bowl. It is very easy to make a mistake that could ruin your design, so don't rush yourself.

Shade around the outside of the dragon design with a small spoon point nib on a medium-high temperature setting. This will guarantee that the dragon is much more distinct against the wood and gives the design a better visual impact, as well as creating a boundary for the paints to be used.

Extend the shaded area out away from the border that you have just created. You can now use a broader nib to shade the surrounding area at the base of the bowl as the dragon outline is protected by the previous work with the smaller nib. A dotted edge can help to create a fading effect.

Swap back to your small spoon point nib and drop the temperature to a low-medium setting. You can then dab the lip of the nib at various points around the body of the dragon to give a textured impression of scales. Work around the whole of the dragon until you are happy with the result.

Use a paintbrush and a scrap piece of wood to experiment with the iridescent wood paints. This will allow you to test and decide on a color scheme by establishing which color combinations work well together before you start working on your bowl.

Carefully paint the dragon at the base of your bowl in your chosen color. I opted for a traditional green dragon (with a flickering red tongue), but the choice is yours. The burned shading around the dragon's body is resistant to the paint; this makes the application of the color an easy process.

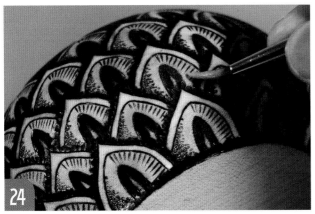

Use different colors for each unique area of the scales on the outside of the bowl. The color scheme that I chose resembled a peacock's feathers, which I felt was an appropriately bold look for a dragon egg. I used an iridescent turquoise paint for the main body of each scale.

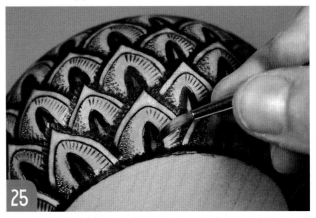

I added a flash of rich, glistening purple paint to the central ridge of each scale. This added a bold contrast to the turquoise color, and the iridescent quality of the paint meant that the surface was starting to look very dramatic when rotated to view from different angles.

The outer lip of each scale was finished off with a coat of electric blue paint. Take care as you work your way around the bowl during all paint application stages so that you don't accidentally smudge or smear any of the colors into each other and ruin your hard work.

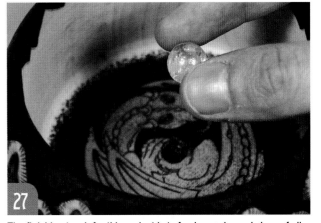

The finishing touch for this project is to feed your dragon's love of all things shiny by adding a crystal, gemstone, or marble clasped within his claws. If your bowl doesn't have an existing depression where the gemstone can be glued, you can drill a few millimeters into the wood to create one.

The Finished Results

Your dragon egg can now be safely used to protect your precious things . . . just be careful not to wake the awesome little beast within! If you want to add a protective finish to your bowl, consider using a spray lacquer or something similar to avoid reactivating the surface of the applied paint in any way that will alter your work.

Castle Kitchen Container

Patterns on page 163

I am a big fan of altering the appearance of items through pyrography to give them a light-hearted or whimsical new appearance. I bought a blank spaghetti container at a craft demonstration event many years ago but had never quite decided what design I wanted to decorate it with. Following a visit to Windsor Castle with my family, I was reminded of my childhood obsession with all things medieval and realized that the shape of the container was perfect to make a castle tower, complete with turrets, "arrow slit" windows, and a solid wooden door.

The most exciting prospect with a design like this is the way that you can customize it completely to suit your own personal preferences. For example, a portcullis would be a perfect alternative to a wooden door if you wished. Windows can be added in a range of different sizes or shapes and in whatever quantity you so desire. You could really go to town and add heraldic flags, carved decorative gargoyles, family crests, or other similar images. The possibilities are endless! Take your time with planning your own design and you will create something unique and extremely special.

The principles used in this project could be used to decorate a range of different wooden boxes or containers, turning them into structures or buildings from any country or period. You could create a range of such containers to hold tea, coffee, and sugar so that they look exciting when lined up together on the kitchen worktop. Another potential idea would be to use the same principle to decorate penholders or desk organizers so that you build a miniature town on your work desk. Just look at the item you plan to decorate and do some research to see what you can represent from its form and dimensions. Let your imagination run free!

Equipment Needed:

- Pyrography machine of your choice and a selection of different pens/nibs
- Round wooden kitchen container/box with lid
- Pencils, sharpener, and eraser—you can use a mechanical pencil if you prefer
- Ruler, circle template, and compasses
- Cardstock, cutting mat, and scissors/scalpel
- Sheet of wood veneer (preferably dark in color)
- Masking tape and wood glue
- 4 decorative miniature brass hinges
- Wire wool or sandpaper
- Superglue

Measure the circumference of the container and divide it into an equal number; 20 is a good figure to work with. This measurement will form the height and width of each section of the battlements in the tower. Cut a square out of the cardstock at that size and use it all the way around the container.

Use your ruler to draw lines across the top lip of the container to form the depth of the battlements and create a 3D effect. Align each opposite mark on the sides and draw a line across the top lip, working your way around the whole box.

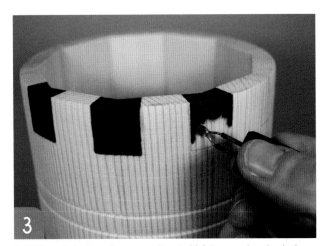

Use a broad shading nib on a medium to high temperature to start shading in the gaps of the castle battlements. Shade on the sides and the corresponding sections of the top lip. You will start to build up an impression of the battlements as solid structures as you fill each alternate square.

Carefully cut a large arched door shape from the sheet of wooden veneer with a scalpel. Ensure that the grain runs vertically from top to bottom of the door shape. Use of a darker veneer gives you a readymade contrast of materials to differentiate the door from the surrounding "wall."

Draw around the veneer door shape on the side of the container to confirm where it will be positioned once fixed in place. If you have used the grain of the veneer appropriately, the door itself should be able to fit the curved form of the container without cracking or breaking.

Add a dark band of shading around the drawn door shape on the container. Use a broad shading nib on a medium-high setting and work out from the outline in an irregular manner. A neat line isn't necessary for a rough area of shadow, and a random approach gives it a perfect finish.

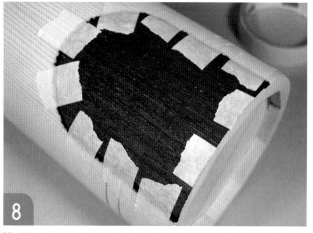

Apply a layer of wood glue to the container and fix the veneer door to the surface. Make sure that you follow the instructions for your chosen make of glue to get the best bond possible. Some brands recommend allowing the glue to dry slightly for a short period before pressing both items together.

Masking tape can be used to hold the door securely in place while the glue is drying. This is particularly important due to the curved surface, as the veneer can lift away from the container if not fixed down. Use several small pieces around every edge and press the tape down firmly.

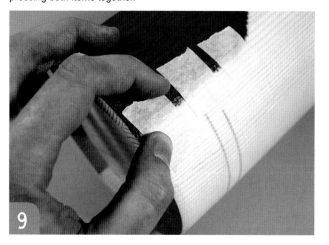

Once the glue has been given enough time to fully dry, carefully remove the masking tape from the veneer. Complete this with caution, as the delicate veneer can be easily damaged if the tape is removed in a rough manner.

Add a series of vertical lines at regular intervals across the surface of the veneer door. This gives the impression of the door being made of many separate planks. A bladed or writing nib on a medium to high heat is perfect for this task.

Use your pencil to draw an archway of bricks around the edge of the veneer door. Use photographs of actual doorways for inspiration or guidance if needed. The bricks should look irregular and uneven to enhance the feeling of age that we are trying to achieve.

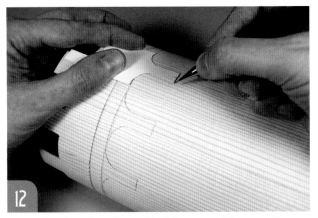

Cut another shape from the cardstock to represent the supporting stone arches under the turret of the castle tower. The shape itself is simple as you can see from the image here. It does, however, start to look extremely realistic when repeated at regular intervals all around the container. If your container doesn't have a grooved line to work to, mark out your own horizontal line around the box.

Design your own "arrow slit" window shape on a piece of cardstock and cut it out carefully using a scalpel. Remember to look at photos of real castle windows for ideas if it helps. This stencil will allow you to add the window shape quickly and easily wherever you want to use it in your design.

Hold the window stencil in position on the container and draw around the inside of the aperture in pencil that you have cut out to recreate the shape on the surface. Repeat this as many times as you see fit around the container itself until you are happy with the number of windows to burn.

Use a fine shading nib such as a small spoon point to burn the shape of the window forms that you have drawn. Work at a medium to high temperature to make the windows dark for maximum contrast. Fill in every window shape in turn until they are all completely shaded.

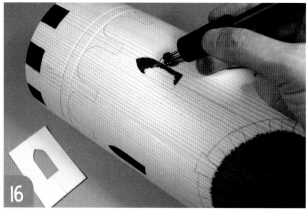

16

Repeat the same process to create windows of different shapes for variety if you wish by making more stencils and applying them in the same manner. In my featured design, I added a row of simple arches above the arrow slit windows to represent another floor of the castle tower.

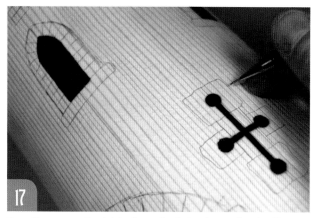

17

Draw the surrounding bricks for each window in pencil, using the same approach as you did for the archway around the main door. Again, these do not need to be regular or identical, as they would have been made by hand in medieval times . . . no mass production techniques back then!

18

Use a fine or bladed nib to burn the lines of the window bricks into the wood. Work your way around the container until every window outline has been successfully completed.

19

Add some dark shading for definition around the base of the tower turret. I've made the most of the decorative grooves that were included in the container blank that I used. You can draw your own detailing in by hand if your box doesn't have any such adornment already in place.

20

Shade the banded section with some rough stippling to create a gritty texture. The bowl of a small spoon point nib at a fairly high temperature is just right for this purpose. Work quickly in a dotting motion for an irregular surface pattern.

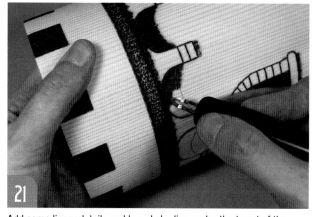

21

Add some linear details and broad shading under the turret of the tower to build up the definition. Using a large area of shading in this way helps to give the visual impression of depth in that the turret substantially overhangs the main body of the tower.

Castle Kitchen Container 99

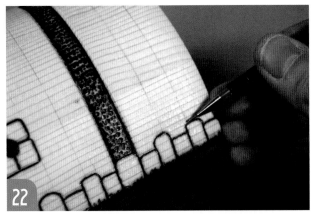

Add a series of horizontal lines around the whole container to prepare for creating the main brickwork pattern. The lines should vary in how far apart they are as this will ensure that the bricks do not look uniform in appearance. Use your finger as a running guide, or wrap a long piece of cardstock around the outside of the container as a straight edge to work to.

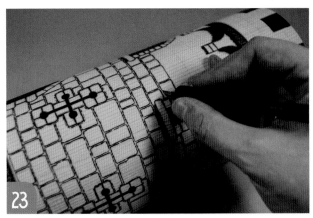

Start to draw bricks of different widths between each horizontal line. Don't worry about how straight or even the lines are, and make sure the corners are not perfect right angles. This will all help to add more character and irregularity to the appearance of our castle!

Work your way up the entire container in this way until all the brick outlines are finished. Don't forget to work across the top lip as well so that the 3D appearance of the battlements is completed appropriately.

Add dark stippled shading to the lower left corner and edges of every brick to start giving an impression of shadow. Work quickly with your spoon point nib's bowl to give a dappled effect; a medium to high temperature gives the best effect.

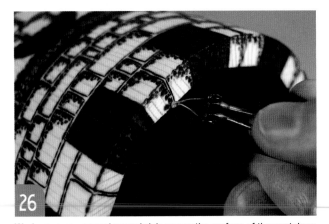

Work your way around every brick across the surface of the container except for those around the door or windows, since those will be given a different finish to make them stand out. Remember to add this texture to the bricks of the battlements on the top lip as well.

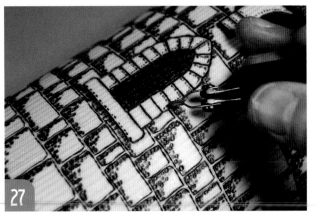

Add a few dotted details to the top right corners of the bricks around the door and windows, using the fine tip of a spear point nib for example. This allows for different contrast to be created across the design and accentuates features like the window arches and ledges.

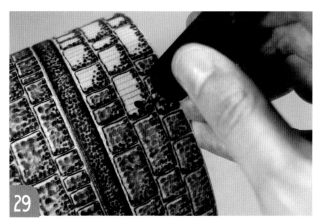

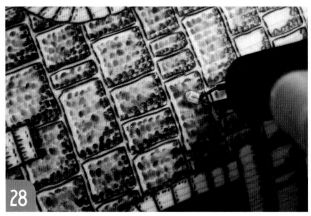

Use a broad shading nib on a medium setting to complete the shading on the rest of the bricks in the wall. If you leave the opposite top right corner and edges unshaded, a subtle highlight is added to the bricks, which enhances the textural 3D appearance we are creating.

Continue with this until every wall brick is shaded. This section of the design does take some time, but the effect is worthwhile. Use a rapid dabbing motion with the shading nib to give a dappled shading effect that recreates the look and feel of roughly carved stone.

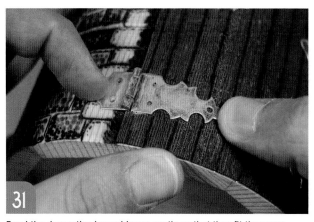

Finish the battlements of the turret by using the same application of texture to the top lip of the container, ensuring that no brick in the wall is left unshaded.

Bend the decorative brass hinges gently so that they fit the curve of the container. Before securing them in place with superglue, you can use either wire wool or sandpaper to distress the surface of the metal. This ensures that they don't look too shiny and out of place on our medieval castle.

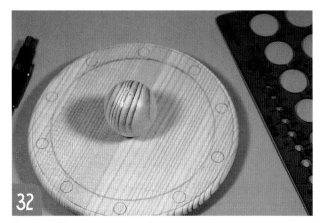

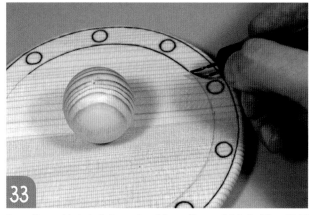

The round lid of the container will be decorated to resemble a medieval shield. Use a pencil and circle templates to create a border with round studs at regular intervals. Complete research online or in books into examples of historic shields to help you create a design if needed.

Use a fine or bladed nib to mark out the outline and detail of the shield border, working at a medium to high temperature setting.

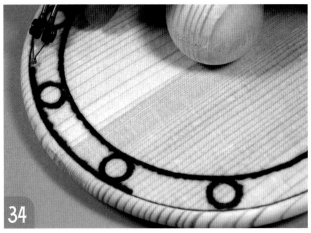

34

Start to shade the shield border with a dark edge for definition and contrast, working around the inside of the border's outlines before shading the outside of the round studs. A small spoon point or shading nib is ideal for this purpose.

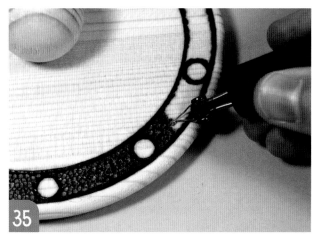

35

Use the round bowl of the spoon point nib to create a texture like that of beaten metal by working very closely and leaving no gaps between each dotted mark. You can see that the pine that my container was made from burned very easily and displayed this texture very successfully.

36

Add an area of shading around the central handle of the lid in the same way as the border. Work carefully if your handle is spherical, so that you do not accidentally burn the handle with the pyrography pen while trying to navigate the narrow gap between it and the lid surface.

37

Draw several straight parallel lines across the main area of the shield to represent the wooden planks that form the surface. Burn the lines with a fine or bladed nib at a medium-high temperature so that they are bold in contrast with the surface itself. These don't need to be perfectly straight.

38

Turn the temperature down to a low setting and use the same fine bladed nib to draw delicate lines randomly in one direction down each "plank." This gives the effect of the grain of the wood. Work lightly and make the lines as natural and uneven in appearance as you can. Also add some random shadow lines to the metal studs around the shield as shown.

The Finished Results

Your castle container is now ready to defend your kitchen from any invading enemies! If you decorate more than one such item for display, you can create a miniature worktop fortification that will be sure to attract the attention of any royal dignitaries or noblemen that happen to visit for a cup of tea.

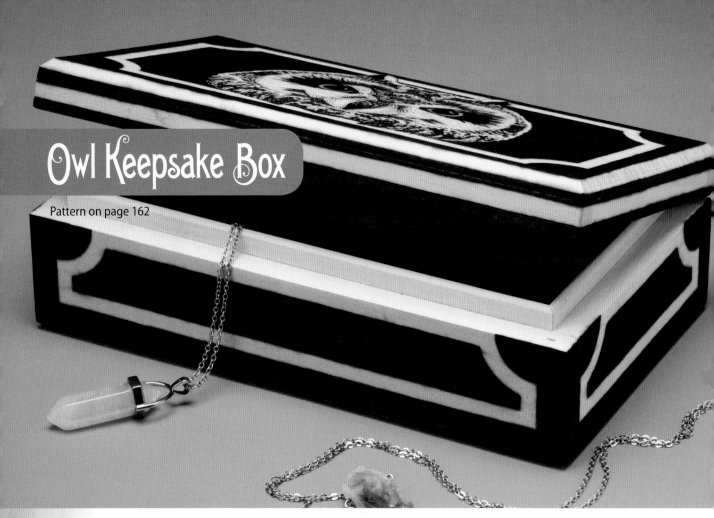

Owl Keepsake Box

Pattern on page 162

Animal portraits are a very common request for any craftsperson, and there is no exception from this if you are a pyrographer. Pet owners adore their pets and love to commission special designs to commemorate this fact. I've made many pet portrait plaques while selling pyrography designs, and it is always a challenge to accurately portray the character of an individual pet from a photograph. I've also been selected on several occasions to make items in the memory of a cherished pet that has passed away, which is always an honor due to the love that is clearly shown toward the beloved animal friend.

Another aspect of pyrography that is always popular is the incorporation of images of wild animals on various items. Most people have a favorite animal of choice and may collect objects on which that preference is depicted. As well as the tigers, elephants, and eagles of this world, I've always been a huge fan of the native animals commonly found in the United Kingdom. Many of my designs have featured badgers, hedgehogs, mice, foxes, swans, frogs, bees, and much more. One of my absolute favorites, however, has always been the owl; they have such a wise and worldly expression and are so beautiful in flight. I'm very fortunate to live in an area where it is not uncommon to see owls in flight while traveling at night.

The short-eared owl featured on this design was adapted from an image taken by a local wildlife and landscape photographer, Angela Norman. I've used the face of this owl to decorate a keepsake or trinket box that can be used to keep small precious belongings safe and protected. My style of animal portrait pyrography as displayed in this project focuses on a very textural approach that makes an ideal introduction to the art form, particularly if you have always been daunted by the prospect of recreating the beautiful yet complex features associated with them.

Equipment Needed:

- Pyrography machine of your choice and a selection of different pens/nibs
- Wooden trinket or keepsake box
- Computer, printer, and paper

- Pencils, sharpener, and eraser—you can use a mechanical pencil if you prefer
- Ruler and circle template
- Tracing paper, scissors, and masking tape

- Bottle of yellow ink and a fine paintbrush
- 4 adhesive cork pads

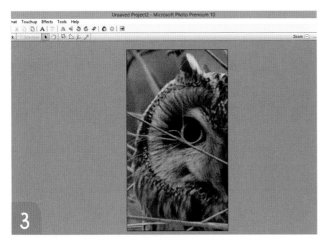

Use a pencil and ruler to measure out and lightly mark a central line vertically on the lid of the black keepsake box. This will form the mirror line that the owl's face will be constructed around. Draw it as softly as possible so that it can easily be erased once it is no longer required.

Open the original photograph that you are using and zoom in on the face of the chosen animal. If needed, rotate the image slightly so that the face is centrally positioned and level on the screen. Select the half of the face that appeals to you the most with a rectangular highlighting tool.

Copy and paste the highlighted half of the animal face into a new image template. Adjust the size of this image so that it is nearly the same size as the depth of the blank box lid you are going to burn it into. You'll need to leave ⅜" to ¾" (1 to 2cm) on either side of the face, so keep that in mind when resizing the image.

Cut a piece of tracing paper to the required size and start to trace the basic structure of the owl face in pencil. Focus on the key areas of darker shadow and tonal change, as well as any areas of distinct texture or other marks that will help you to construct the facial features in pyrography on the wood.

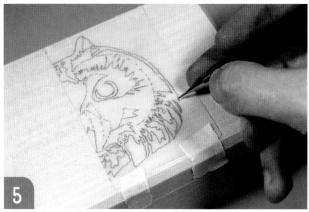

5

Secure the tracing paper into position on the box lid with the traced lines facedown on the surface. Carefully draw over each of the lines on the reverse of the tracing paper in order to transfer them all onto the wood. Once done, remove the tracing paper with caution to avoid ripping it.

6

Turn the tracing paper over and place it back onto the wooden surface so that the second half of the owl face aligns exactly with the one that you have already transferred. Fix it in place again with masking tape to avoid unwanted movement.

7

Scribble firmly with a pencil on the reverse side of the tracing paper to transfer the other half of the design onto the box lid. Do not press so hard that you damage the tracing paper or the box lid itself. Remove the tracing paper carefully when complete so that you don't smudge the design underneath.

8

You should now have a fully transferred owl face design on the box lid, ready for the application of pyrography to make it permanent on the surface. Now is the time to make sure that there are no mistakes or problems with the design, as it is difficult to make corrections once burning has begun.

9

When starting with the face of an animal, I usually begin with the main "solid" features with a defined outline. On this owl, this meant burning the eyes and beak with a small shading nib at a medium-high temperature setting. Keep the outlines of these areas as neat and sharp as possible.

10

Leave a small unshaded area in each pupil to create a reflected highlight for realism. Start to shade in the areas of smooth black tone within each pupil and then form the areas of shadow that surround each eye. Keep the tone as even and dark as possible, as this will really make these features stand out.

Turn the shading nib around in order to use the fine edge for the sharp lines surrounding each eye. Flick the nib to make lines that fade to a defined point and closely follow the pencil lines in order to create the curved linear features. Refer to the source image regularly to check your accuracy.

Move the nib around again so that you're using the flat, broad area to completely shade the remaining area around each eye. You should now have defined each of the eyes fully to ensure that they will stand out as the prominent features of the entire design. Realistic eyes are a must in any portrait.

Use a fine or bladed nib on a medium temperature setting to add finer linear texture where needed. Keep the longer lines as fluid and smooth as possible by moving your pen in a single curved motion, rather than stopping and starting to create the line in several separate sections.

Use the tip of a shading nib on a medium-high heat setting to build up the areas of soft smaller feathers, making random dappled marks with a quick repeated dabbing motion. Fill the relevant textured areas in this way, working carefully to replicate the markings to the best of your ability.

Turn the temperature setting down and start to build up the medium tonal values of the lines radiating out from the shadowed areas around each eye. Work quickly to avoid leaving marks that are too dark, and move the pen in a smooth curving motion to recreate the direction of each mark accurately.

Keep the temperature setting at the same level and start to make more dappled marks for the soft feathers in the areas that you previously created in step 14. As you add these medium tones in the various areas of feather textures, the different sections of the face will start to join as a single image.

17

Add the areas of softer medium texture using the bowl or flat edge in a soft flicking motion of broader strokes, rather than the distinct lines created when you use a sharp edge or tip. Lifting the nib quickly from the surface at the end of each flick will give a graduated fade to the marks.

18

Continue to spread the soft, darker feathers around the outer edge of the face with the dabbing motion of the shading nib tip. Adding these marks closely together will give a darker effect, while spreading them apart creates lighter areas of texture. Refer regularly to your source photo to remind yourself of what you are working to represent.

19

Dragging the tip of the nib slightly rather than simply pressing it in the dabbing motion will create the effect of slightly longer feathers that are not as round in shape. This is useful for the texture at the lower side of the face where the feathers are more individually distinguishable due to their position.

20

Reduce the temperature setting of the pyrography machine and add marks by using a similar motion for depth and texture. Due to the lower heat, these marks will not be as dark in tone and will, therefore, start to add more definition and pattern to the feathers surrounding the main facial area.

21

Use the lip of a shading nib on a low-medium temperature setting to add flowing lines around the central area of the face. These can be irregular and scratchy since this will add to the random natural characteristics; however, focus on the direction of each line as this will build up the structure of the face.

22

Add yellow ink with a fine paintbrush to the area around the pupil of each eye to represent the golden color seen in the photograph. Using just a hint of a bold color in a design like this can really add a dash of vibrancy to the whole image. It can lift the entire picture to a whole new level.

Now that the main burning of the owl face is complete, lightly construct a border around the box lid using a pencil and ruler. Draw a pair of parallel lines evenly spaced around the lid on every side to form a rectangle that goes underneath the owl face, as this adds a sense of depth to the design.

Use a circle template to add a curved section at each corner of the rectangular border. This creates a border that is elegant and with increased visual appeal. Take every effort to keep the border as crisp and accurate as possible so that the geometric design looks perfect to the eye.

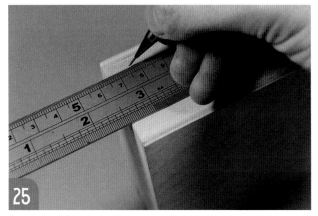

Use the pencil and ruler to draw an identical pair of tramlines around the edge of the box lid. These lines should flow smoothly around all four sides and, ideally, be the same distance apart as the border on the main box lid. Drawing them this way will ensure that the design is visually cohesive and pleasing to the eye.

Use a fine or bladed nib at a low-medium temperature setting to draw the outlines of the border on the main box lid. Remove the unwanted pencil lines with an eraser after burning. Take the burned border outlines close to the owl image, but make sure not to touch the edges of the face.

Add a protective shaded area around the edge of each border outline. Work your way carefully around the side of the owl's face, leaving a soft and uneven white highlight around the edge rather than burning an unrealistic dark, solid line; this will help to give the impression of soft, downy feathers.

Change to a broad shading nib on a high temperature setting to block in the solid, dark areas left on the surface of the box lid. A larger shading nib enables you to cover an area of smooth shading much more quickly than a small nib, but it does require a higher heat setting due to its size.

Once the main box lid is finished, turn the box onto its side and add the outlines of the corresponding border around the edge of the box lid with a fine or bladed nib. A medium heat setting should be enough to make a crisp line without any scorches or heat flaring.

Complete the shading on each edge of the box lid with the broad shading nib on a high temperature setting. Work your way meticulously along each borderline, taking care not to inadvertently cross over into the unburned border that you are striving to create. Keep your hand steady as you burn.

Draw out identical geometric borders on the sides of the main box compartment to match the existing design on the box lid itself. Make sure that all the dimensions are identical and that the borderlines are spaced in a way that corresponds precisely with the lid design.

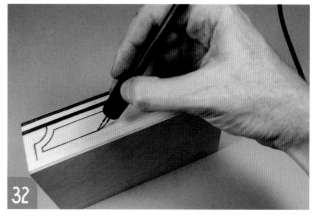

Burn the outlines that you have just constructed on the sides of the main box compartment by using the fine or bladed nib in the same way that you created them on the previous sides. Remember to keep the lines as straight and neat as you can; support your hand as you burn if that is necessary.

Use the broad shading nib again on the high temperature setting in order to add the flat area of dark, even shading within and around the new border outlines. Pay special attention when shading into any right angles with the broad nib. Turn it slightly to one side if needed to prevent any errors.

Once all shading is completed on every panel, turn the box over and attach an adhesive cork pad in each corner of the base. This will protect any furniture that you stand the box on from any accidental scratching, as well as lifting the box slightly away from any surface that it is placed upon.

The Finished Results

Your elegant, yet simple keepsake box is now complete, with the watchful eyes of the owl protecting any treasured possessions placed within it. If you wish, you can develop other designs by creating more complex and varied borders behind your selected animal portrait of choice.

Set List Text Art Frame

Patterns on page 164

I have always found lettering and fonts a fascinating subject to create decorative designs with. The vast range of potential styles available means that there is almost a limitless scope for creativity. There is a font out there for every occasion or purpose. Bringing this into your pyrography designs can lead to extremely exciting results even when used with no other form of decoration or imagery. I regularly make picture frames as commissions for special occasions such as births, weddings, anniversaries, graduations, and more. The focus of such designs is always the lettering used to add the personal dedication to the recipients, as this is what makes the design unique and personal to them. In this project, I've taken that principle to the next level by using a wide range of different fonts and lettering styles to make a piece of art.

As a huge fan of rock bands and live music, I am also a collector of set lists, those pieces of paper taped to the stage to help the band with the songs they have chosen to play that night. They are a perfect memento of a great gig, as they are often limited in number, a challenge to get hold of, and therefore a desirable piece of memorabilia to any fan. I decided to make a piece of "text" art based on the fantastic set played by talented American musician Scott Sorry and his band at the legendary 100 Club in London, combining a range of different fonts to represent each song that he played that night in February 2017.

You can use the approach that I have utilized here to make your own personal piece of "text" art, perhaps to immortalize a concert that you have fond memories of. Alternatively, you can apply the same principles to any lettering concept you wish to create using pyrography, such as a list of favorite songs, a poem, a dedication to a loved one, a bespoke message, and much more.

Equipment Needed:

- Pyrography machine of your choice and a selection of different pens/nibs
- Blank wooden frame
- Piece of birch plywood (sized to fit within the frame)

- Computer, printer, and 8½ x 11 (A4) paper
- Pencils, sharpener, and eraser—you can use a mechanical pencil if you prefer
- Ruler and scissors/scalpel

- Masking tape and tracing paper
- Cardstock

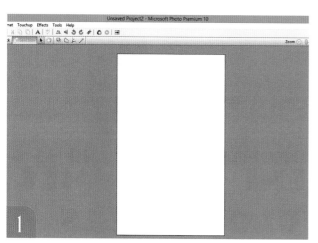

Create a template on your photo editing software at the exact dimensions of the aperture of your chosen frame.

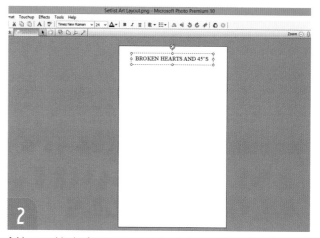

Add a new block of text containing the first song title or line of your word art design.

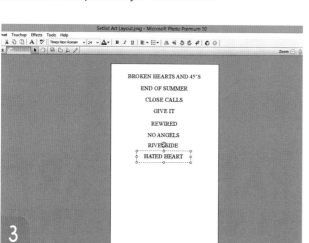

Continue to add each block of text in sequence to build up the content of your design.

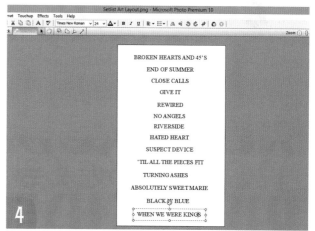

Add the final block of text, ensuring that you now have all that you need in the correct sequence. Explore the various fonts available to use, identifying options that are visually strong and suit the look that you are trying to create.

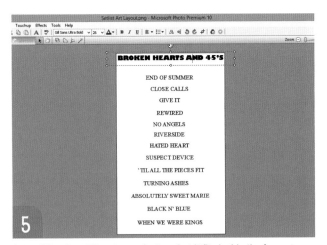

5 Amend the size of the chosen font so that it fits inside the frame as fully as possible.

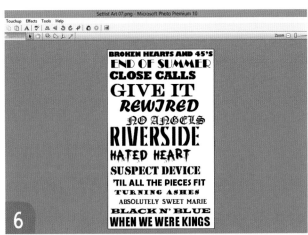

6 Continue this process until you have selected a different font for every block or line of text. Save the file that you are working on as a .jpg version, since this flattens the image. You cannot edit the text after doing this save, since it is now simply a part of a "picture."

7 Select the first line of text using an appropriate highlighting tool. Cut it and immediately paste it back in the same position, before resizing it so that it fills the width of the background.

8 Continue to cut, paste, and resize each line of text, moving them up closely to each other as well to remove any gaps between the rows.

9 Work your way down your page, resizing and repositioning every line of text to fill the area as much as possible.

10 You can also stretch the lettering vertically to maximize the amount of space that is used; some fonts can be improved greatly this way.

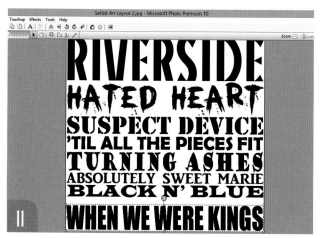

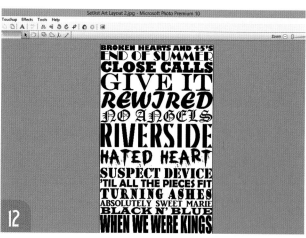

Position the last line of text at the very bottom of the visible area so this will give you an idea of how much space you have remaining to fill.

Once you have adjusted all of the lines of text, the whole area within the working template should be completely full with no leftover space and all lettering neatly aligned at the edges of the page.

Print a reversed image of the layout for easier tracing and transferring. Measure the exact height and width of the printed lettering, break the design down into sections, and prepare an identical rectangle with the same dimensions in the center of the plywood that will go into the frame.

Working through the design in sections makes it more manageable. Trace one of the middle sections first, focusing on a few rows of lettering at a time. This reduces the chance of smudging any of the traced lettering while you work on a nearby row.

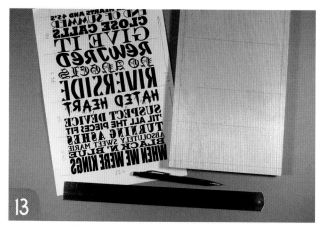

Position the first section of traced lettering in the corresponding rectangle that you have marked out on the plywood. Secure it firmly in place with masking tape prior to transferring it to the wood. Use small pieces of masking tape, ideally with a piece at each end of every row of lettering.

Use a pencil to transfer the letters to the wooden surface by outlining them with a scribbling motion. Work on one row at a time, transferring just one block of lettering before removing the masking tape and cutting the used section of tracing paper away to give access to the wood below.

Use a fine or bladed nib on a low-medium temperature setting to burn the outline of the lettering into the wood as crisply as possible. Keep the lines as fluid as possible. Turn or reposition the wood regularly if needed so that your hand is always working at a natural, relaxed angle.

Once you have completed burning the first block of text, transfer the next row by scribbling on the tracing paper, taking care not to press too hard as this can leave an indentation in the plywood. Cut the used paper away after removing the masking tape.

Burn the outlines of the newly transferred text with a fine or bladed nib. If the lettering itself is also fine, you can use the same nib to block in or shade the lettering as you go. Save any large or chunky areas of text for later in the process.

Once you have completed all lettering in the first section that you transferred, you can trace the adjacent sections onto tracing paper and secure them in place in the same way. Make sure that the lettering is positioned in place exactly where you want it in relation to what you have already burned.

You can experiment with different marks or textures to represent it rather than always using solid outlines for your lettering. For the stencil font in this image, I used a stippled effect of fine dots with a spear point nib to make it look like the lettering had been spray-painted.

For this font that resembles freshly painted lettering, I used a fine nib at a medium-high temperature to make irregular lines in the direction of each line that forms the letters. This gave a textured finish to the lettering, which is reminiscent of thick paint strokes, particularly where they overlap.

23 Once those sections have also been transferred to the wood and burned in, trace any final remaining blocks of text onto the tracing paper and securely fix them in place with masking tape in order to finish the whole process.

24 Nibs with a very fine point can be used to immediately shade or color in smaller lettering rather than trying to draw an outline first. Take care to remain within the pencil marks in order to keep the lettering neat and precise.

25 Once all lettering has been marked out successfully using pyrography, use an eraser to remove any visible pencil marks or layout lines before you continue shading the lettering. Fine sandpaper can always be used for any stubborn areas of pencil that an eraser struggles to remove.

26 Carefully use a spoon point nib at a medium-high temperature to block in some of the fonts. You can use the bowl of the nib to shade wider areas, and the lip of the nib to work into any narrower or finer areas without ruining the outlines.

27 Experiment with different shading techniques to add variety and interest to your text art design. For this font, I shaded the top half of the lettering only, leaving a soft transition of shading into the bottom half by flicking the spoon point nib's bowl gently off the wood.

28 Shade one letter very dark before dropping the temperature to create a paler tone for the following letter. Repeat throughout one whole row.

29

Draw pairs of parallel lines diagonally across a taller font, and shade around them to create a plain stripe of unburned wood within each letter.

30

There is a wide range of techniques that you can use to add variety to your lettering. These include stippling dots within a border, or softly shading the letters from dark at the top and bottom in a gradual manner so that the middle of the letters is unburned across the whole row.

31

For this larger line of text, I created bands of dark tone that gradually reduced in size as they moved downward in the letters. This added a bold visual pattern to catch the eye, instead of blocking the whole letters with a more uniform shading technique.

32

Apply the same process to create the layout for the frame as you did for the text art itself. Create a template that replicates the exact dimensions of the wooden frame and prepare the layout of your lettering to achieve a successful composition. Add shapes such as stars in the corners if needed.

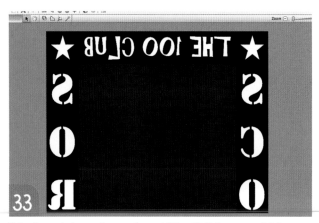

33

If the frame is larger than a piece of 8½ x 11 (A4) paper, print the composition in two halves at the exact size that you require. The layout will be too small to work from if the printer resorts to a default setting where the printed image is adjusted to fit the page.

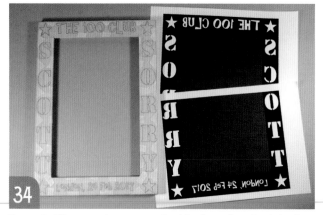

34

Trace all of the separate components of the frame layout onto tracing paper and secure them in place around the frame with masking tape.

35 Transfer small sections of the layout onto the wood by scribbling on the back of the tracing paper, taking each section one at a time and burning it before moving on. This will ensure that your design is transferred as neatly as possible without any errors or problems.

36 Work your way around the whole of the frame in this manner, completing the design in sections until the outline is complete across the entire piece. Use a fine or bladed nib at a low-medium heat setting to make the sharp outlines for each letter or shape.

37 Once the outlines are completed, start to create a protective shaded border around each letter and shape using a small spoon point nib or similar. This will ensure that you do not inadvertently go over your outlines by using too large a nib; this can eliminate fine detail or ruin your lettering.

38 Once each letter and shape has had a shaded border placed around it, you can use a larger or broader shading nib to shade the areas between each word. These can require a high temperature setting to work most efficiently due to the larger area of surface contact with the wood.

39 Mark a borderline in pencil on the side of the frame and then shade around the edge to fill in the area that you have indicated. This allows the design to make use of the whole area visible, rather than only utilizing the front face itself.

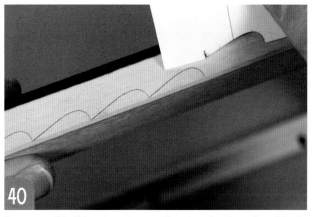

40 Draw a small half-teardrop shape on the edge of a piece of cardstock and cut it out using a scalpel. You can then use this to draw identical repeated shapes along the edge of the frame. This will resemble a saw blade to fit in with the "punk" feel of this design.

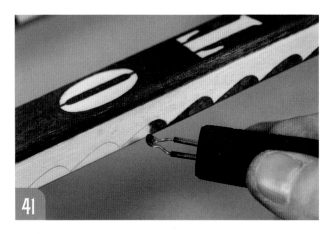

41

Shade each section of the saw blade pattern with a broad shading nib at a medium-high heat setting. As you fill in each individual shape, the visual effect of the saw blade will begin to emerge. The possibilities are endless for this approach. It is a handy way to create a regular repeating pattern.

The Finished Results

Your text art is now ready to be fitted inside its frame and hung on display. This technique can be used for a wide range of decorative purposes and is especially suited to making special, meaningful gifts for a loved one. You may very well soon be creating your own gallery of framed text artwork.

Children's Reward Bank with Tokens

Patterns on page 165

I am a big believer in encouraging children to understand that working hard and helping others is something to be rewarded. This is particularly true in an age when our society is so much more focused toward the virtual world and the avenues for instant entertainment that it provides. Children should be praised for a job well done around the house, achieving a good result at school, or some other accomplishment. This reward doesn't always have to be financial, either, particularly if money is tight for the family.

This project was conceived as a way of rewarding a child for such efforts in a manner that also encourages them to value the effort of saving up what they have earned. The reward bank has been made using the principle of a money box, but with tokens that the child can accrue over a longer period.

I've designed several different tokens so that the parent can reward achievements or results at an appropriate level. An easy household chore may earn a small token, while a substantial accomplishment at school with more effort involved would result in a greater bonus. The child could then save these tokens up in exchange for an agreed treat or prize.

The theme I used in this project was based around the idea of a retro radio alarm clock with a few additions used to represent this in a light-hearted manner. The tokens were designed to fit in with the theme of music so that they tied in with the design on the money box. The joy of such a project is that the theme or appearance of the item can be tailored to suit the likes or hobbies of the child that will be using it.

Equipment Needed:

- Pyrography machine of your choice and a selection of different pens/nibs
- Wooden money box blank
- Quantity of assorted small wooden shaped blanks (to be used as tokens)
- 5 small wooden discs (to be used as buttons)
- Computer, printer, and paper
- Pencils, sharpener, and eraser—you can use a mechanical pencil if you prefer
- Ruler and circle template
- Tracing paper and masking tape
- Marker pen
- Colored inks and paintbrush
- Hand drill and center punch
- Wood glue and superglue
- Small telescopic/extendable metal antenna

Mark up a border around the edges of the moneybox. These should be on the top face and around all side panels. Use a pencil and ruler so you only make light lines that can easily be erased at a later point. Make all lines the same distance from the edge. I worked to a 3/16" (5mm) gap.

Burn each of the border outlines using a fine or bladed nib on a low-medium temperature setting. Use the nib evenly and steadily across the surface of the wood so that the lines are as neat and crisp as possible with no flaring or scorch marks.

Fill in the borders using a small shading nib. Work away from the lines that you have drawn and try to make sure that you do not accidentally go over them by mistake. Work your way around the whole box to create a consistent and even dark border.

Lightly mark up a rectangle on the rear of the moneybox using a pencil and ruler. I rounded the corners of the rectangle that I drew in order to fit in with the shape and form of the box itself. This will form a decorative panel on the reverse of the moneybox.

5

Neatly and carefully draw the outlines of the rear panel into the wood with a fine or bladed nib in the same way that you did the previous border outlines. Take special care if you are creating tightly rounded corners with a bladed nib. Try to use the very point of the nib in a tight radius.

6

Add another line 1/16" (2mm) from the existing rear panel, which will be used to help add some depth and definition. Add more detailed elements, such as circles, in each corner to represent screws holding the panel in place.

7

Use your fine or bladed nib to burn these lines into the wood and add detail to the screws. Create a shadow effect for the panel by only outlining the bottom and right edge to be shaded. The top and left edges will then be left plain to represent a highlight in contrast with the darker opposite edges.

8

Fill in the shadow of two panel edges using a small shading nib on a medium-high temperature setting. These lines are only 1/16" (2mm) apart, so work very carefully to only shade within the lines. Use the lip of a spoon point nib to give a better chance of an accurate and neat finish.

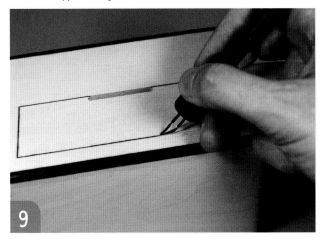

9

Add a rectangle to the top panel of the moneybox, incorporating the slot where the tokens will be inserted. This will form the clock display of the moneybox. Draw the rectangle first in pencil before burning the lines in with a fine or bladed nib.

10

Add a surrounding border to the clock display outline, again using parallel lines approximately ⅟₁₆" (2mm) from those that you have already burned. Keep these lines as neat as possible by working carefully with your fine or bladed nib, doing your best to create sharp and smooth marks in the wood.

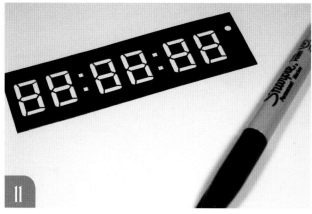

11

Print the clock display pattern at an appropriate size to fit the area that you have created for it on the top face. Reversing or "flipping" the image on your computer before printing it will make it easier for you at the tracing and transferring stage. Have a black marker ready for the next stage.

12

Block in the areas on the printed pattern that will not be showing as "illuminated" in your clock display. The remaining areas of the digital display will form the numerals that you have selected; remember that you are creating a reversed image and will need to read backward from right to left.

13

Trace the reversed numerals onto tracing paper ready to be transferred onto the wooden moneybox. I chose 07:20:18 to represent the item being made in July 2018, but you may wish to choose something meaningful to the recipient, such as a date of birth or special anniversary.

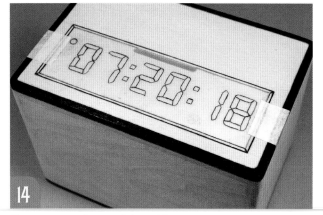

14

Place your traced numerals in position on the wooden box inside the border you have burned with the tracing paper facing downward onto the surface. Secure it in place with masking tape so that it remains in place without moving during the transfer process.

15

Scribble carefully on the back of the tracing paper so the numerals you have prepared are transferred neatly onto the wooden surface. Be careful not to press too hard as this can lead to unwanted indentations in the wooden blank.

Start to burn the numerals by working around the outside of the traced lines with a small shading nib. If you prefer to do so, you could always use a fine or bladed nib to draw their outlines first before you start shading around them.

Once the area immediately surrounding the forms of the numerals is completed, you can swap to a broader shading nib to block in the dark areas more quickly and efficiently. The larger the nib, the more surface area is in contact with the wood and, therefore, the quicker you will shade an area.

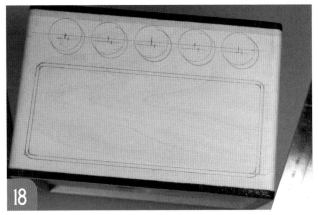

Now you need to create the layout for the front of the radio alarm clock. You will need to prepare a panel to represent the speaker, as well as adding five buttons for the controls. Draw one circle for the button position and then add an offset identical circle for its shadow.

Use a fine shading nib, such as a small spoon point, on a medium-high heat setting to block in the area of shadow under each button. The shadow area will only be visible as a small crescent of darker tone once the wooden button adornment is glued into position over it.

Complete the outline of the panel for the speaker using a fine or bladed nib at a low-medium setting for maximum crispness and accuracy. Remember to take care when creating any rounded corners so that the lines are as smooth and fluid as possible.

Add a pattern of circles for the speaker panel texture. You can do this by drawing a grid and adding circles with a template at regular intervals. Alternatively, keep your eyes peeled for impromptu stencil templates, such as this black plastic insert from a microwave meal that I have upcycled.

Children's Reward Bank with Tokens 125

22

Shade around the circles of the speaker section with a small spoon point nib at a medium-high heat setting to create a dark area of tone interspersed with small, round unburned areas. Take care not to go over any of the border outline as you have at other stages during this design.

23

Reduce the temperature setting to a low-medium heat and use the same nib to fill in the small circles within the speaker panel. Build up the tone carefully so that the circles are dark but do not blend in with the surrounding area; otherwise, they will be indistinguishable, and the effect will be lost.

24

Add some areas of decoration to the side panels of the radio alarm clock in keeping with the style or theme that you want to create. I chose images to represent a punk-rock theme, such as an electric guitar. I've also used the Eric logo of the band The Idol Dead with kind permission of the members!

25

Draw the decorations lightly in pencil first before burning them with a fine nib. You could always trace images on if you do not feel confident drawing freehand. The aim here is to make the decorations look like stickers that have been stuck on the side of the radio alarm clock.

26

Once you have burned the sticker decorations into place, draw a pencil line around them if you want them to be protected by a plain white border. This also helps them to visually stand out from the texture that is to be added shortly around the sides of the box.

27

Adding the texture around the whole of the box is possibly the most time-consuming part of this project. Use a writing nib on a medium temperature setting and draw small, irregular shapes to give the impression of a textured leather surface or similar; just doodle away around each panel!

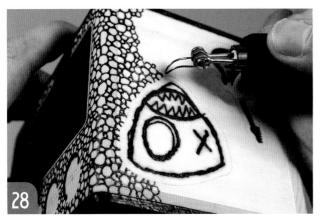

28

Continue the pebbled leather texture seamlessly around the whole box, working right up to the border of any panels. When you are working around the sticker designs, stop at the pencil line you have drawn to leave that plain white border you prepared earlier.

29

Gradually you should work your way around every side panel of the radio alarm clock until the texture joins up at the point where you started. It's a slow process, but the decorative result is well worth it. The pattern is visually striking as well as also being very tactile, inviting you to touch it.

30

Draw the symbols onto your control buttons. I chose those regularly used to represent power on/off, rewind, play/pause, fast-forward, and stop functions. Burn them in carefully with a fine nib, such as a bladed or spear point. Use caution when working on small items so that you don't slip.

31

Apply a small amount of wood glue to the back of each control button and then press them firmly into position before allowing them to dry. Remember to position them so that the burned shadow effect you created earlier is not covered up in error.

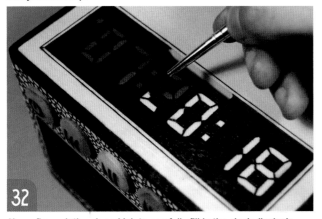

32

Use a fine paintbrush and ink to carefully fill in the clock display's numerals with a color of your choice. I chose a vibrant red ink and applied several layers to make the color on show as vibrant as possible. You could use any color that you prefer . . . but the brighter, the better!

33

Use the same process of ink application to add some exciting color to some of the sticker designs if you wish. A small flash of color can sometimes be all you need to lift a pyrography design, so the maxim of "less is more" applies here. Consider carefully where and how you wish to use inks.

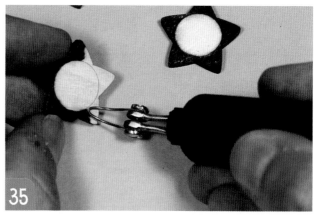

Add a basic decorative border to one side of the circular reward tokens by pressing a fine nib into the edge of the wood repeatedly, rotating the blank to work your way all around it. You can make the pattern uniform and consistent if you wish, or work in a more random and irregular manner.

On the star-shaped reward tokens, I used a circle template to add a circle to the center of each before shading the points of the star in an even, dark tone. The unburned circular section can then have a value or symbol added to it to show what reward level it represents.

Either draw or trace a series of numbers or symbols onto each reward token to show the value of them. I added a bit of variety by using some musical notes on my smaller tokens alongside the numerical worth of each.

Burn the numbers and musical notes into each token using a fine nib, such as a spear or blade. Remember to work carefully while holding small items, as your fingers will be close to the hot nib while you burn. The opposite side of the "larger" discs is now ready for a special decoration.

On the five-point tokens, I created a small CD motif. Draw the design onto the blank, add the main structural lines, apply some dark shading, use a lighter tone for the background, and then finally add some finishing detail around the edge and center. Repeat this design across all tokens of this value.

A vinyl LP design was added to the ten-point tokens. Using a series of close concentric circles drawn with a bladed nib, some dark shading was then applied before a few additional lines were added to give the sense of the disc being covered in grooves. Repeat this again and the tokens are finished!

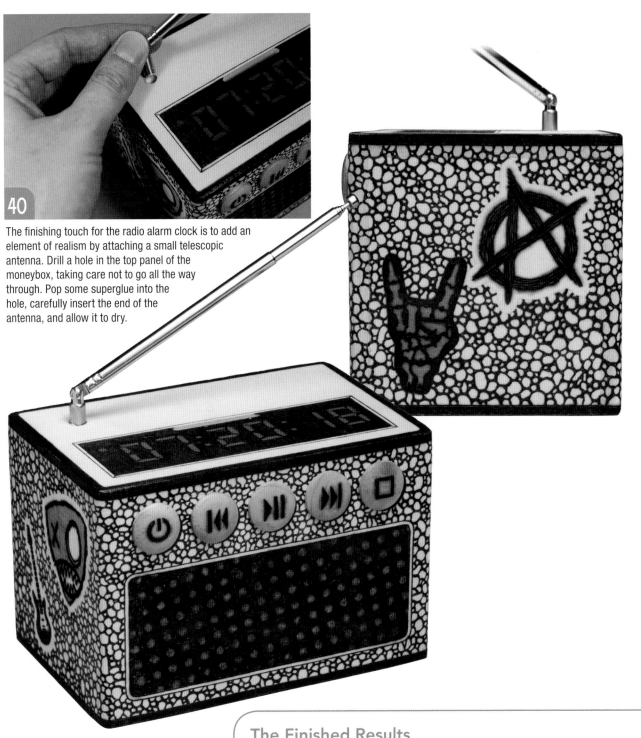

40

The finishing touch for the radio alarm clock is to add an element of realism by attaching a small telescopic antenna. Drill a hole in the top panel of the moneybox, taking care not to go all the way through. Pop some superglue into the hole, carefully insert the end of the antenna, and allow it to dry.

The Finished Results

The moneybox is now ready for its young owner to start filling with tokens that demonstrate how hard they have worked or how helpful they have been. With careful consideration and planning, you will be able to develop a range of concepts to suit the personality or interests of any potential recipient.

Christmas Eve Platter for Santa

Patterns on page 162

Christmas is a time of year when homes all over the world are adorned with a vast array of festive decorations in celebration of the special time. As a result of this, Christmas itself provides an immense source of inspiration to artists, makers, and craftspeople, irrespective of what media or materials they work in. The scope for ideas is almost infinite in scale and variety, making it an extremely popular occasion creatively.

I've made many Christmas designs over the years, including festive tree decorations, plaques, coasters, gift tags, key rings, and many more. I was asked to make my first Christmas Eve platter in 2017, and this started me thinking about how to create one that was unique to my Wood Tattoos style of pyrography. I wanted to make something that combined all of the traditional imagery of the festive period with a contemporary twist. The idea of children leaving a drink and a snack out for Santa Claus and his reindeer to keep them refreshed during their busy Christmas

Eve activities was an appealing idea, and I decided that creating something special to help with that family tradition could result in a treasured item being made that would bring joyful anticipation when it was brought out each year before Christmas Day itself.

I decided to use a bark-edged (or waney) plaque, as it also reminded me of the traditional Yule log. These rustic plaques look amazing when a pyrography design is applied to them, and I used mine as the basis for a layered design by adding some smaller bark-edged coasters into the composition. These form the central focus of the ceremony around leaving the drink and snack of choice out before bedtime. I developed an exciting festive border to decorate the body of the plaque itself in a vivid and exciting fashion. Due to the materials and decorative approach used in this project, no two items can ever be identical, so I hope you enjoy bringing your own creativity and imagination to your endeavor.

Equipment Needed:

- Pyrography machine of your choice and a selection of different pens/nibs
- Large waney/bark-edged plaque, sanded on at least one side
- Two small round waney/bark-edged coasters, sanded on both sides

- At least one festive shaped plywood blank or similar
- Computer, scanner/printer, and paper
- Pencils, sharpener, and eraser—you can use a mechanical pencil if you prefer

- Tracing paper, masking tape, and scissors
- Bottles of red and green ink
- Fine paintbrush
- Wood glue

Mark out the rough location of your extra blanks by drawing lightly in pencil on the surface of the bark-edged plaque. You can draw freehand if you wish. I found some bangle blanks and a napkin ring to draw around the inside of as a guide since these were smaller than the blanks themselves.

To create your own decorative scroll, draw a swirl shape (as pictured) at one end of the plaque. This will form one edge of the scroll. Alternatively, find and trace a scroll design from the Internet or a pattern sourcebook if you prefer to do so.

Trace part of the scroll as shown and place it horizontally a few inches (several centimeters) across the plaque's surface from the initial swirl. This will become the other opposite side of the scroll once all of the lines are appropriately joined together.

Join the opposing sides together using lines that are gently curved to enhance the sensation of old parchment paper. You can join the lines with a ruler, but this gives a more regular appearance to the scroll image.

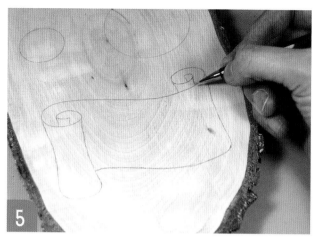

5

Add the short lines to show the edges of the paper where the scroll curls back in on itself. This simple technique has easily created the sensation and appearance of an old parchment scroll with very little effort at all.

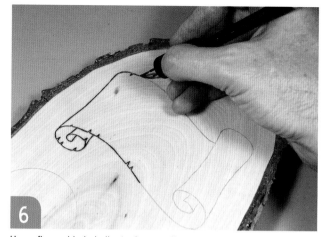

6

Use a fine or bladed nib at a low-medium temperature setting to burn the outline of the scroll. Add a few V-shaped notches of different sizes sporadically at irregular intervals around the outline to give the impression of rips and tears in the antique paper scroll.

7

Lightly draw out your personalized message or poem for Santa Claus in pencil on the scroll. You can use a computer font if you wish for a neat, precise look. I used a more natural, childlike style of handwritten lettering to represent the young person writing the note themselves.

8

Burn the lettering into the wood using the point of a fine or bladed nib on a medium to high heat setting. The lower coil of the scroll can be saved to add the name of the child or children to the design if you wish in order to personalize the piece as a bespoke commission.

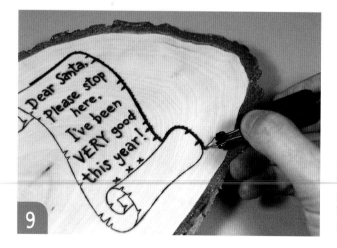

9

Use a small shading nib, such as a spoon point, to shade around the edge of the scroll as a protective barrier of shadow. As well as protecting the detail that you've already created from mistakes, this will help to add a sense of depth against the other components of the pattern to be used.

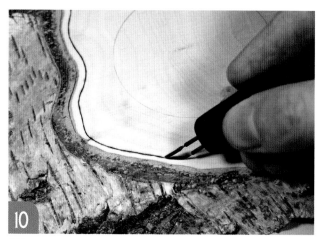

Add an outer border to the main surface of the plaque using a fine or bladed nib on a medium temperature setting. I followed the grain of the wood to give an impromptu, naturally irregular border, utilizing the unique character of the wood to my advantage.

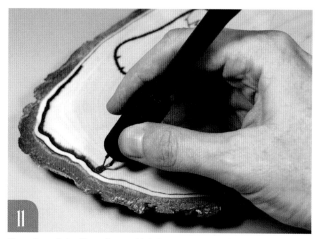

Use a broad shading nib on a high temperature setting to shade within your outer border. This will protect the crisp outline that you have created and build up that sense of depth mentioned previously. Work away from the outline for a small distance only; around ⅛" to ³⁄₁₆" (3 to 4mm) is perfect for this.

Draw out your first decorative festive element onto a piece of tracing paper. I chose a ribbon bow for my initial component. Turn the tracing paper over and carefully draw over the initial outlines to transfer the image onto the wooden surface.

Flip the tracing paper over and draw the image again in another position around the plaque to add the element elsewhere. Repeat this process three or four times in order to use the same image in several places around the decorative border.

Use a fine or bladed nib to burn the outline of each element neatly into the wooden surface, working your way around every transferred drawing in turn. Try to make the lines as neat as possible so that the images are sharp and tidy in appearance.

Add a protective shaded border around each of the burned elements, in an identical way to the one that you added around the scroll previously. Use a small shader or spoon point nib, taking care not to go over the burned outlines into the image itself.

Draw your second festive element onto tracing paper. I used a sprig of holly leaves and berries for my next addition. Draw it onto one side of the tracing paper, flip the paper over, and position it on the wood. Draw on the rear to transfer the holly leaves onto the wood.

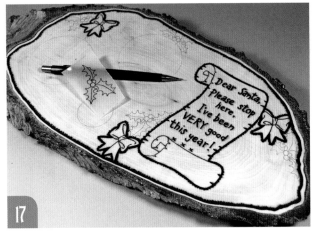

Repeat the process of tracing and transferring in order to add the image in various places around the border. Again, use it in around three to four different locations across the surface. My approach was to gradually work outward from the initial elements in order to fill the space as much as possible.

Use the fine or bladed nib to create the outlines for your second design element in the same way as you did for the first elements. The burned outlines will end wherever they meet a protective shaded border to give the impression of the second element sitting below the first.

Use the small shading nib to again create an area of protective shaded border around the outside of each second design element. These shaded areas will join together where they meet other similar shadows and will start to build up a cohesive background pattern of jumbled festive images.

Repeat this same process of tracing, transferring, outlining, and shading the third festive element. You can see that my third image was a jolly snowman, complete with hat and scarf! As you add each progressive element to the border, you will work your way toward filling all available space.

Continue this process through a succession of separate festive elements as you gradually cover all available space except where the coasters and shaped blanks will be added. I've used a selection of images that include festive candles, candy canes, stars, Christmas presents, and traditional bells.

At some point, you will have filled so much of the background border that there are only small spaces left to cover. Go back through your various tracings and see what you can use to fill these areas, such as the tip of a single holly leaf or one end of a festive candy cane treat. Burn them in!

Very simple shading will now be added to this design to give it some depth and variety. Use a small shading nib, such as a spoon point, on a low heat setting to add the first of two different tonal values to the designs, adding definition, depth, and difference to each design element in turn.

Continue the soft layers of shading around the whole decorative border, adding shadow and tone to bring each image to life. Add shadows where a sense of 3D form is required, such as around the folds of the bows, inside the festive bells, and within the curled-up shape of the scroll itself.

Christmas Eve Platter for Santa 135

25 Keep the same shading nib attached but turn up the temperature setting on the pyrography machine in order to start adding darker lines, shadows, and tones to the designs for areas, such as the snowman's hat, patterns on the presents, texture on the holly leaves, and the form of the bells.

26 Continue this approach with the second level of shading across the whole design, including adding more definition and shadow to enhance the 3D appearance of the scroll. The entire pattern of the border should now have a warm and rich sensation of tone and texture across it.

27 Time to start on the decorative coasters next. Add a border outline to the main face of both bark-edged coasters to define the area that will be decorated. Use a fine or bladed nib in order to create a crisp line around the whole edge as you did with the main plaque itself.

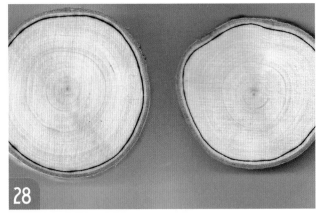

28 Use a scanner to scan the surface of both coasters so that you can prepare the text and decoration to be added to them. If you do not have access to a scanner, you can always prepare the decoration freehand or by tracing and transferring the separate elements.

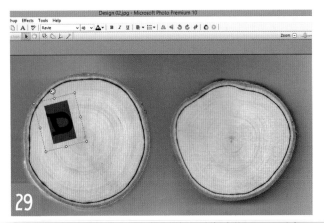

29 Select an appropriate font and start to lay out the letters separately in turn. This will enable you to change the position and appearance of each letter individually, rather than treating them as a word and relying on the default horizontal positioning and spacing associated with regular typing.

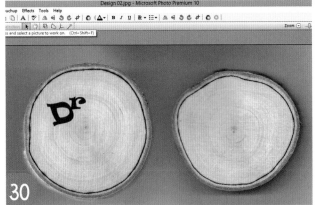

30 Start to add each subsequent letter in turn and adjust the size or position as you go. This will give you a more random and slightly haphazard look to the text, which is more in keeping with the sense of fun and excitement that we are trying to create.

Follow the circular form of the coasters by arranging the letters in rough semi-circular arches. The word "Drink" arches over the top while the word "Santa" curves around below it in the opposite way. Use larger letters for the main words and smaller letters for the central "for" text.

Once you have completed the layout for one coaster, you can use the "Select All" function to highlight every single letter element before copying and pasting them over to the second coaster for the basis of that item as well.

After pasting the copied items onto the second coaster, remove the word "Drink" so that you can add the word "Snack" in its place. This will help to give both coasters a similar visual appearance and save you a lot of time that would be needed to start the second coaster from scratch.

Use the same principle of construction and layout to add the word "Snack" to the second coaster. Add the letters in a similar shape or structure to the approach you used on the first coaster so that they appear identical in style.

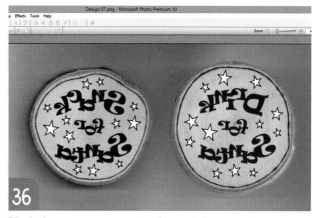

Add a selection of star shapes at random intervals around the words on each coaster. Change the size and angle of each star to create visual interest and variety. You should only need around a dozen stars on each coaster to fill the surrounding space.

Flip the image on your computer prior to printing to speed up the tracing and transferring process. Remember to print the page at the exact size setting if you have used your scanner so that you know the design will be ready for application to your coasters with no adjustments necessary.

Trace the lettering and star shapes onto tracing paper with a pencil, ready to be transferred onto the surface of the corresponding wooden coaster. Repeat the process for the design on the second coaster.

Cut each tracing out carefully with a pair of scissors so that it can then be taped in place on the wooden coaster blank. Use masking tape to hold it in place and prevent any unwanted movement during the transferring process.

Scribble on the back of both tracings in order to transfer the design successfully onto the wooden surfaces. Press firmly to make the design as visible as possible, but take care not to press so hard that you go through the tracing paper or damage the smooth surface of the wooden blank.

Use a fine or bladed nib to start the burning process by creating the outlines of the stars first. As these blanks often require you to work across the end grain of the wooden blank, you will probably need at least a medium temperature setting in order to get a smooth and distinct line.

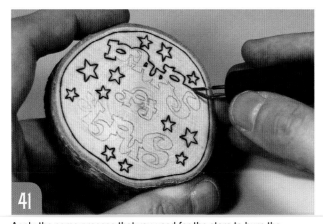

Apply the same process that you used for the stars to burn the outlines of the letters. Take extra care to ensure that the points where two lines meet are precisely completed. The lettering can be ruined if two lines cross incorrectly through lack of attention to detail.

Use a small shading nib, such as a spoon point, to gradually shade around the outline of each star and the associated lettering. Use the sharp lip of the shading nib to carefully shade between any areas where two lines meet at an acute angle. Take care not to stray over any of the outlines.

43 Once the solid shading around the text and stars is complete on each coaster, use the flat surface of a shading nib (or the bowl of a spoon point) to shade the remaining background in a stippled, dotted manner. Dab the nib repeatedly around the wooden surface to build up an area of textured tone.

44 Use a fine paintbrush to delicately apply green ink to one of the words on each of the coasters. If needed, add a few separate coats of ink to make sure that the color is as vibrant as possible. Take care not to drip colored ink anywhere else on the wooden design as you work.

45 Repeat the process with red ink on one of the remaining words after thoroughly cleaning the paintbrush of all traces of green ink. It seems most fitting to color the word "Santa" with the red coloring! Complete the same process on both wooden coasters.

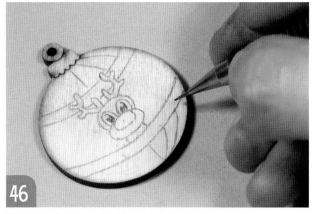

46 The small shaped festive blank will be used to create a resting place for a carrot to be fed to Santa's reindeer! Lightly draw an appropriate reindeer-themed design in pencil onto the surface of one of the blanks. Feel free to look for ideas online or in books, or copy the simple design I've used here.

47 Use a fine or bladed nib to delicately create the outlines of your reindeer decoration. The tip of the nib can be used to block in areas of fine, dark shading if needed, such as the eyes, nose, and antlers of the reindeers featured on my bauble. Remember to leave Rudolph's nose free of shading, though!

48 Festive blanks, such as those featured here, are often made of thin plywood or something similar. If you want to increase the height of the place for the reindeer snack, glue two or more identical wooden blanks together with wood glue and allow them to dry.

49

Add some color to the reindeer bauble by using the same green and red inks that you applied to the drink and snack coasters. As well as adding another point of visual interest to the design, the matching colors will help to indicate where items are to be placed when the design is in use.

50

Once the coasters and festive blanks are dry, apply a fine layer of wood glue to the large wooden plaque and firmly press the additional small blanks down into place. Keep the pressure on them for a few minutes to ensure a firm bond has been made before placing the design safely to one side to allow it to dry.

The Finished Results

This Christmas design is now ready to grace your festive fireplace or mantlepiece for many years to come. I cannot guarantee that it will increase the quality of the gifts that Santa brings to your children . . . you'll have to say that they still need to work hard and make sure that they remain on his "nice" list for that to happen!

Reversi Game Board and Counters

Patterns on page 166

Reversi has always been one of my favorite games since childhood. Simple in concept yet difficult to master, this game of strategy is a battle between two players across an 8 x 8 game board. The counters are double-sided in color, with one side "dark" and the other side "light." The winner of the game is the player that has more of their counters facing upward once the board is full. Each player takes their turn to place one of their counters face up on an empty square to capture and flip their opponent's playing pieces over by enclosing them in a straight line, with the game constantly evolving as the numbers of dark and light counters change during the battle for the upper hand.

Making a reversi game board is a simple concept for a pyrographer. All that is required is a sufficiently large playing board of 64 squares and at least 64 double-sided counters; it's always a good idea to have a few spare pieces in case any get lost. The counters are traditionally circular in shape, but you can decide to choose something completely different if you prefer. I decided to use star-shaped wooden blanks for variety, but the same principles apply to whatever you select.

My design concept for this project was to combine the traditional appearance associated with pyrography with a contemporary feel by using contrasting modern materials. Through incorporating the likes of chrome and Perspex® (acrylic sheet), I have made a design that is not only pleasing to the eye through the combination of differing textures, but also something that is inherently durable, long-lasting, and hard-wearing. The patterns and shapes that I have used can be changed to suit your own preference, so please do feel free to simply use the principles of this project as a launchpad for your own unique design!

Equipment Needed:

- Pyrography machine of your choice and a selection of different pens/nibs

- 70 Shaped small wooden blanks (to be used as counters)

- 64 Wooden square blanks (ideally 1⅜"–1½" [35–38mm] wide at most)

- Large piece of birch plywood (15¾" x 15¾" [40 x 40cm] is ideal)

- Large piece of clear Perspex/acrylic sheet (exactly the same size as the large piece of plywood)

- Pencils, sharpener, and eraser—you can use a mechanical pencil if you prefer

- Cardstock, cutting mat, and scissors/scalpel

- Ruler, circle template, and compasses

- Masking tape, wood glue, and superglue

- Hand drill and center punch

- 4 ³⁄₁₆" (5mm) metal spacers

- 4 Decorative chrome drawer handles (with appropriate nuts/bolts/screw cup washers as fittings)

Add any linear detail to one side of your playing counters with a fine or bladed nib. My plan for the star-shaped counters was to have one heavily decorated "dark" side and to leave the "light" side completely plain for maximum contrast.

Add areas of dark shading for definition on the playing counters. Marking the sections to be shaded with a quick dot is a good way of making sure that you don't make any errors by filling in an area incorrectly, which can be very frustrating when trying to make all 70 counters identical.

You can make a different area of shading by simply using a series of parallel lines with a bladed nib. I used the form of the star-shaped counters by adding lines that followed the direction of each point, which give it a 3D feel across the decorated face.

Use cardstock to prepare a template to be repeated across each playing square, drawing the pattern with pencil and any other necessary equipment, such as compasses. I chose a design based on an old Celtic church window. Cut the design out carefully and precisely using a scalpel.

Use the template to draw the pattern onto every separate playing square. I used a circle template to draw the two concentric circles first, before using the handmade stencil to add the final detail to the pattern within the smaller circle. This can take some time but ensures your patterns are identical.

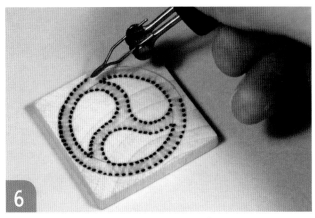

6

Use a fine nib, such as a spear point, on a medium temperature setting to start filling in the pattern on half of your playing squares. Work inside the lines as neatly as you can to keep your pattern precise. You may find it easier to complete the outlines first.

7

Once the outlines are completed on 32 of the playing squares, start to use the same mark-making technique to evenly fill in each pattern with dots for shading. This can be a time-consuming but relaxing process! You should now have completed half of the total quantity of playing squares.

8

For the remaining 32 playing squares, you are going to shade around the outside of the pattern for contrast. Use the same stippling technique as you did previously, but work on the other side of the pencil lines that you have drawn for each pattern to build up an image in the negative.

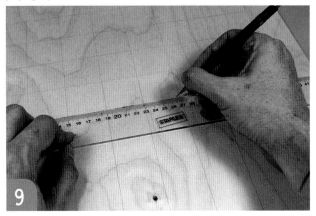

9

Draw a grid on your 15¾" x 15¾" (40 x 40cm) plywood board to create the 8 x 8 playing board using a pencil and ruler. The aim of this process is dividing the whole wooden board up into 9⁄16" (4cm) squares with the outer perimeter forming a border around the playing area itself.

10

Mark the center point of each of the four corners using a pencil and ruler. These points will be used for joining the two large plywood and Perspex sheets together once the making process is complete and you are ready to begin full assembly.

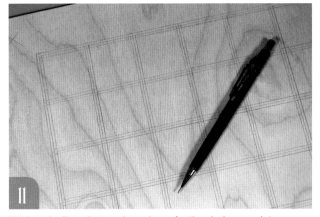

11

Thicken the lines that you have drawn for the playing area into more substantial borders by drawing another line ¹⁄₁₆" to ⅛" (2 to 3mm) away on both sides of the existing marks. This identifies the areas that you will be shading to fill the gaps between the playing squares you have already made.

12

Complete a neat lined border on the very outside edge of the playing area with a fine or bladed nib at a low-medium temperature setting. Try to keep the lines as smooth and straight as possible so that the board looks crisp and well-finished.

13

Use a broad shading nib to fill in the playing square borders marked out in pencil. Take care not to stray over the edge that you have created in the previous step, but it does not matter if you go over the lines within the playing area as the squares themselves will be glued down over the top.

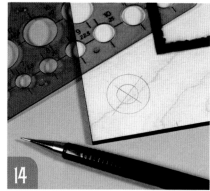

14

Mark out where the metal spacer rings will go using a circle template. The height of the metal spacer rings should be the same as the thickness of the playing squares; for my design, both were 3/16" (5mm). This ensures that the playing board will fit together neatly when assembled.

15

Start to build up a pattern of circles along your outer border around the playing area. My plan was to build up an interlinking chain of circles around the perimeter, so I started by drawing 13/16" (22mm) circles on alternating edges of the border where the squares met.

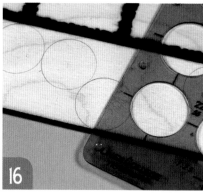

16

Link the previously drawn circles together with more circles of the same size with a circle template. Each circle should touch the two others on either side of it to form a continuous chain that runs around the entire border.

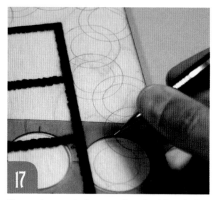

17

Draw a larger circle around each of the circles you drew in the previous two stages. I used a 1¼" (32mm) circle around each 13/16" (22mm) circle to start creating the appearance of a physical chain of rings. Make sure that these large circles are placed centrally around those within it to keep the design even.

18

Start to complete the outlines of the rings using a fine or bladed nib on a low-medium temperature. The aim is to make the rings look like an interlocking metal chain, so work out where lines go over each other or under each other to create this 3D impression.

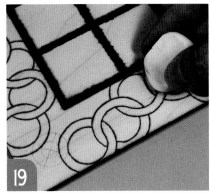

19 Once the burned outlines are complete, work your way around the border with an eraser to remove any traces of unnecessary pencil lines from the chain design before you start shading them in more detail. Leave the markings for the corners in place for guidance when you attach the spacers.

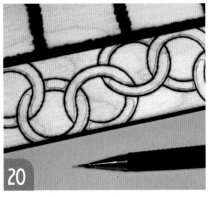

20 Use a pencil to mark out the areas where shading is to be added to the links of the chain. The idea is to add shadow where one link goes under another, or around their forms to create a sense of form. You can do this freehand but do consider looking at real or photographed chains for help if needed.

21 Use a fine shader such as a small spoon point nib on a medium-high heat setting to start adding the dark shadow to the chain links you have created. Take care to stay precisely within the lines that you have already burned in by working out from them with your nib into the center of each "link."

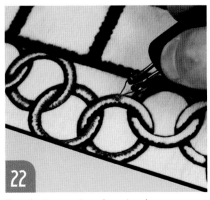

22 Turn the temperature down to a low or low-medium setting and add some softer, lighter shading to the opposite side of each chain link. This starts to emphasize the solid form of the chain and gives it a more realistic appearance. Work your way around the whole border to complete the pattern.

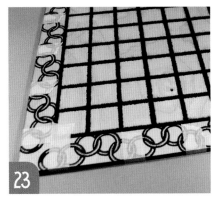

23 Secure the plywood and Perspex boards together with masking tape, ready to drill the four corner holes. If the boards are held together firmly at this stage, all four holes should be perfectly aligned, and this will make the assembly of the finished piece much easier.

24 Mark the point to be drilled in each corner lightly with a center punch so that the holes are accurately positioned. You should be able to do this by simply pressing the center punch with your hand rather than needing a hammer. The plywood is soft enough to not need substantial pressure.

25 Drill each of the four corner holes in turn. Use a drill bit that is the correct size for the bolts that form your fittings. It should be just wide enough for the bolt to go through and no larger to prevent any unwanted movement within the design.

26

Attach all 64 playing squares to the plywood board with wood glue, following the instructions for the brand that you are using. Alternate the squares by design to build up a pattern, mirroring a chessboard of black and white squares . . . your board can now be used for that game, too, if you like!

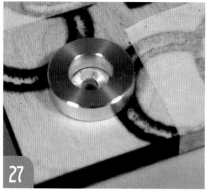

27

After allowing the playing squares enough time to dry securely, place your metal spacers into position in each corner. You can attach them permanently with superglue if you wish to do so; this way they will not move once the board is assembled.

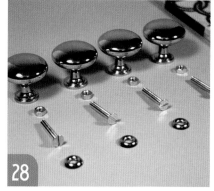

28

Prepare the different elements for each foot of the playing board. In my design, I have used a screw cup washer, a bolt, a nut, and a chrome drawer handle for each corner. There is a wide range of fittings available; see what you can get at your local hardware store to suit your own design.

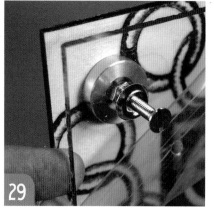

29

Remove any protective film from the inside of your Perspex sheet, and peel back the corners of the exterior film in turn as you start to assemble the feet. I placed the bolt through the cup washer and secured the nut on the inside, where it will sit within the metal spacer between the two layers.

30

After tightening the nut and bolt as fully as possible by hand in each corner, join the plywood and Perspex sheets together fully by attaching the drawer handles to the underside of the board. These will form hardwearing feet that also lift the playing board away from the surface that it stands on.

31

Peel back the remaining protective film from the top of the Perspex sheet and your design is now complete. You can now place your playing pieces in position, ready for your first game of reversi on your new creation.

The Finished Results

This project uses a very simple circular theme as its decoration, but you can tailor the design to suit any idea that you wish. You could make a personalized game for a family member, tailoring it to accommodate something personal or meaningful to them in some way for a unique gift.

Halloween 3D Platter

Patterns on page 166

Creating designs for special events or occasions is an ideal challenge for any craftsperson, and Halloween is an ideal choice due to the vast range of spooky imagery associated with it. You can really let your imagination run wild as you adorn your work with all manner of witches, pumpkins, skeletons, ghosts, ghouls, and much more. For this project, I decided to create something that would be a real centerpiece for any Halloween party or event.

I used a large turned wooden platter made of ash that I had purchased from a gallery many years ago as the basis for this project. It was sitting in my stock of blanks just waiting for inspiration to strike, and this project was the perfect opportunity for it to be brought alive with a creepy Halloween theme. You could create something similar on any number of blanks available through craft suppliers, or you could

always commission a friendly woodturner to make you a piece to your own specifications if you have such a contact.

As well as using a border of silhouette designs that fit the theme perfectly, the main idea that I wanted to apply to this project was a tactile experience through the addition of 3D wooden shapes. I had an idea that the Halloween candy displayed on this platter should look like they were surrounded by disembodied eyeballs floating in a pool of glistening green slime. I thought that this would be a concept that would either appeal to children or make them want to scream when they saw it! Making designs with a playful element to them is such a rewarding experience, whatever the reaction you provoke from the people that use it.

Equipment Needed:

- Pyrography machine of your choice and a selection of different pens/nibs
- Large round wooden platter/dish (ideally with a large flat surface in the center)
- Computer, printer, and 8½ x 11 (A4) paper
- Pencils, sharpener, and eraser—you can use a mechanical pencil if you prefer

- Ruler, circle template, and compasses
- Tracing paper
- Cardstock, cutting mat, and scissors/scalpel
- Iridescent green wood paint/stain
- Paintbrush

- Quantity of half sphere wooden blanks in assorted sizes
- Selection of colored permanent markers with broad nibs (blues/greens/grays/purples)
- Red permanent marker with a fine nib
- Wood glue

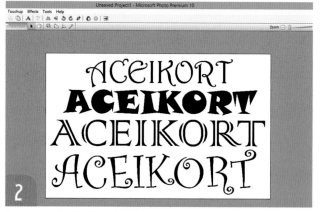

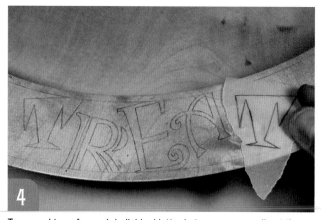

Create a border around the lip of the platter using a pencil with your fingertips as a running guide. Approximately ³⁄₁₆" (5mm) from the edge is a perfect distance. Keep your grip firm and your hand steady as you run your fingertips around each side of the lip to draw two parallel borderlines.

For the words "Trick or Treat," there are only eight different letters that you will need access to, so ignore the rest of the alphabet. Use your computer's photo editing software to select three or four fonts. Choose styles that are wildly different to add a little Halloween kookiness to your design.

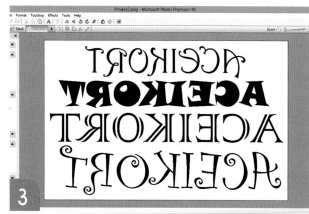

Reverse or flip the image before printing so that it is easier to trace and transfer. Print the image to fill a piece of 8½ x 11 (A4) paper. It doesn't matter if the letters are a little big compared to the platter's lip, as this will add to the chaotic feel of the design.

Trace and transfer each individual letter in turn as you spell out the inscription for the border. Swap fonts after each letter so that you build up a random, disorganized feel. Add each letter at a different angle and don't worry if part of the letter does not fit into the border; the crazier, the better for this!

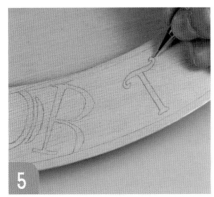

5

If the traced letters are a little difficult to see on the surface of the wood, go over them with pencil until they are clearly visible rather than making your job difficult in terms of burning. Make sure the text fits well around the border. I managed to fit three inscriptions on this design.

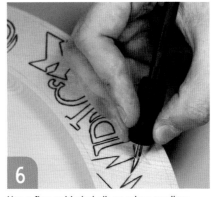

6

Use a fine or bladed nib on a low-medium temperature setting to burn over the traced lettering and create the outlines of your inscription. Stop at any point where the letter outlines touch the pencil border that you drew in step 1 of the project. Aim to keep your burned lines sharp and smooth.

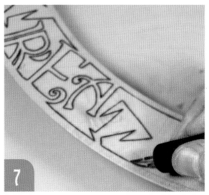

7

It is now time to form the completed border by burning over the pencil outlines and linking them to the points where the letters join them with the bladed nib. This will enable the outer rim to be built up with the letters themselves visible as unburned "negative space" against a burned background.

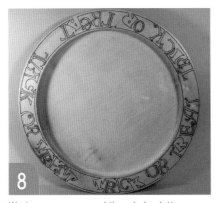

8

Work your way around the whole platter, burning over the relevant pencil marks until every line is linked up with the border. This decorative rim will also act as a frame for the ghoulish centerpiece within. You can also now get rid of any unwanted pencil lines using an eraser before the next stage.

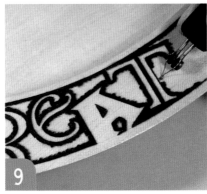

9

Create a dark shaded border around each letter and the edge of the border on the rim using a small spoon point nib or similar at a medium-high heat setting. The letters themselves should start to really stand out in a striking manner due to the contrast between the shading and the plain wood.

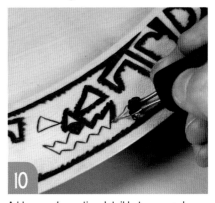

10

Add some decorative detail between each "Trick or Treat" inscription for variety. You can use anything spooky to tie in with the Halloween theme of the design. I opted for three evil pumpkin faces as a simple but effective embellishment to break up the text.

11

Add a border of stippled dots inside the shaded boundary to increase the contrast with the lettering. The bowl of a spoon point nib is perfect for this, or any other small shading nib or writer can be used. Use the nib at a medium-high temperature, press firmly, and work quickly around the rim.

12

Swap over to a finer nib, such as a spear point or the tip of a blade, to continue the dotted pattern but with more precise and smaller dots. This allows you to give a graduated shading effect by introducing more unburned wood and counterbalancing the impact of the dark dots.

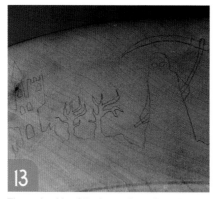

13

The underside of the large platter I used was the perfect canvas for a bold silhouette design. Create one by drawing a continuous scene of creepy figures and scenery; the focus is on visual impact over fine detail. Work to create one continuous and flowing line that forms the edge of the silhouette.

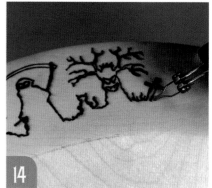

14

If your platter is also large, you may find it easier to complete the silhouette design in segments. Draw a section and then burn the outline with a fine writing nib or spear point. Once you have burned that section, you can start drawing the next section as you work your way around the full form.

15

Keep developing the design around the rim. Incorporate as many frightening elements as you can, including witches, ghosts, pumpkins, spooky trees, gravestones, castles, cats, vampires, zombies, haunted houses, bats, and more. Add occasional blades of grass in various places for detail as well.

16

Create a zigzag pattern using a bladed nib around the lower edge of the platter. This will give a layered effect to the design by adding a white "grassy" foreground over the main area of shadow and is more visually interesting than shading the whole silhouette down to the base in a solid band.

17

Use a small spoon point shader to start blocking in the main features of the silhouette border. Setting your machine at a medium to high temperature will allow you to create a deep black tone that is even in consistency for maximum contrast and impact.

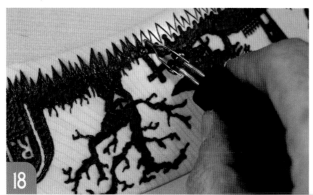

18

Use a spear nib to shade the areas between the zigzag grass pattern that you created. Turning the platter upside down makes the shading process much quicker as you can press the blade in and draw it down toward the silhouette area you have already shaded, filling the remaining areas with tone.

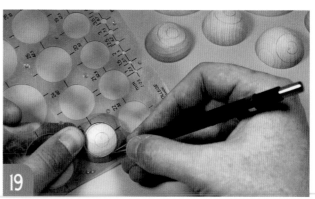

19

Time now to start working on your eerie eyeballs. Use a circle template to draw two concentric rings on each half sphere blank for the pupil and iris of each eye. Add them at different angles and positions so that each eye will look like it is floating in a different way when fixed in place.

20

Place your "eyeballs" in a random arrangement around the inside of the platter. Try not to use any formal structure or pattern so that the anarchic feel is kept up. Lightly, use pencil to draw around each eyeball blank in turn to mark its position and then place it safely to one side for later use.

21

Use a broad shading nib at a high temperature setting to make a shadowy border for the base of each eyeball position. Continue the shading into each pencil circle by several millimeters as well so that no plain wood is visible when the eyeball is later attached in place.

22

Lightly draw a pencil line around the inner lip of the platter to mark out the edge of the gruesome slimy contents that will be on display. This doesn't have to be a neat or precisely measured border, so feel free to work by eye and hand alone when drawing this perimeter line.

23

Add another dark, uneven band of shading along the inside of the perimeter circle you have just drawn. Use the broadest nib you have and work at a high temperature setting in order to create bold marks, flicking the nib away toward the center of the bowl as you work your way around in a circle.

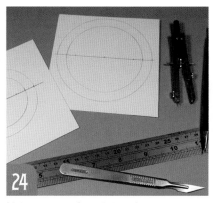

24

Make a couple of "ripple" stencils that will be used to suggest the eyeballs are suspended in liquid goo. Prepare the pattern in pencil on cardstock. Each stencil was designed to be ⅜" (1cm) thick and to leave a ⅜" (1cm) gap around each size of eyeball blank to give a rippling effect of concentric rings.

25

Cut each stencil out carefully using a scalpel on a cutting mat. Do not press too hard with the scalpel as this can cause you to slip. Try to cut the stencil out as precisely as possible so that you get a smooth circle with no flat edges or points when you draw around it.

26

Place each stencil template in position carefully around the relevant size of eyeball blank on the platter. Draw lightly with a pencil around both the inside and the outside edge of the stencil in turn to create two neatly matched rings. This process will gradually be completed around every eyeball blank.

27

Start by completing the ripple ring closest to where the eyeball will be glued. Use a fine or bladed nib at a medium-high temperature setting and draw it slowly around the drawn circle to create a line that is dark and bold. Repeat this around each of the stencils that you have transferred so far.

Halloween 3D Platter 151

28 Turn the temperature setting down to a low-medium setting and draw it around the ripple line furthest away from where the eyeball will be glued. This creates a finer and thinner quality of line to represent the way that ripples fade with distance. Add this effect to the other stencil lines as well.

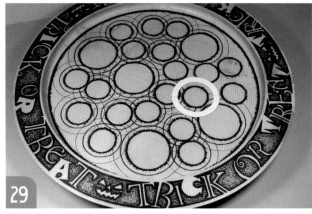

29 Work your way across the surface of the platter using your ripple stencils. It is easier to complete three or four sets of "ripples" at a time so that you do not get too confused with pencil lines everywhere. Draw a few, burn them accordingly, and repeat until you have covered everything.

30 Once the ripples have been fully created, apply a generous layer of green iridescent paint around each eyeball and within the outer perimeter. Add extra coats to get a vibrant and vivid final effect. The green slime should glisten and gleam when it catches the light from various angles.

31 While the green paint is drying on the platter, start work on creating your eerie eyeballs. Use a broad shading nib at a medium-high temperature setting to fill in the dark black area that represents the pupils of each eye first. Repeat the process across every blank until all are completed.

32 Change to a smaller shading nib, such as a small spoon point, and start to create the outer rim of the iris. Work your way around the inside of each circle, creating a solid round rim and dragging your nib in toward the center to create the initial irregular lines within each iris.

33 Use a fine or bladed nib at a medium temperature setting to add radiating lines of varying lengths into each iris, working out from the pupil and in toward it from the opposite edge. Apply the lines at random intervals so that the eyes do not appear too uniform or artificial.

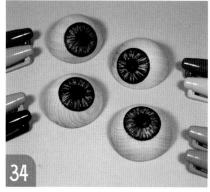

34

Gather your available broad permanent markers for the eye colors and pair them up. Fill in each iris with two similar colors so that the iris looks more natural than if it was filled in with a flat area using a single pen. Use as many color variations as you can to add variety to the whole piece.

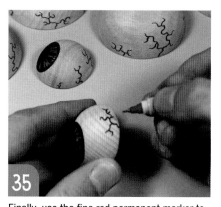

35

Finally, use the fine red permanent marker to add a number of irregular random "veins" at the back of each eyeball. This gruesome detail also introduces another color to the design that stands out against the green slime. Make each vein different by letting your pen see where the hand takes it!

36

Apply a generous layer of wood glue to the back of each eyeball in turn and then press it firmly into place on the platter. Position them as centrally as possible within each area that you have prepared with the shadow and ripples around. Leave the platter to one side to dry thoroughly once all eyeballs have been glued in place.

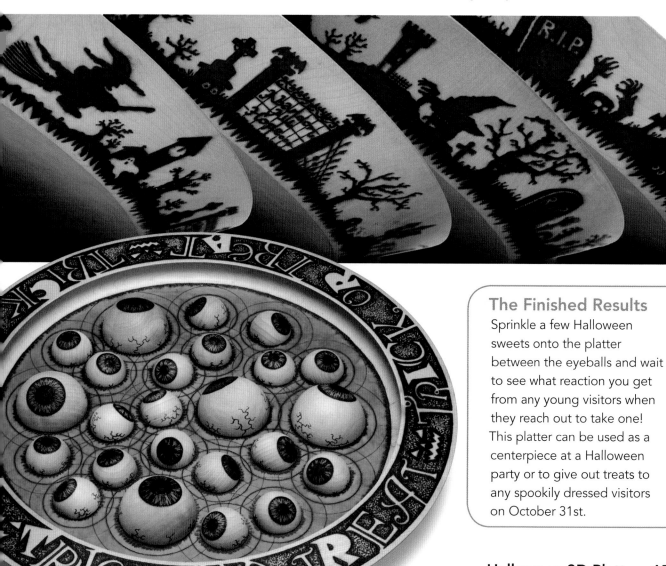

The Finished Results

Sprinkle a few Halloween sweets onto the platter between the eyeballs and wait to see what reaction you get from any young visitors when they reach out to take one! This platter can be used as a centerpiece at a Halloween party or to give out treats to any spookily dressed visitors on October 31st.

Chapter 3: Patterns

Copy all patterns at the size and scale you need to fit your project.

Herb Garden Label Set
(See page 26)

BASIL   *Ocimum basilicum*

CHIVE   *Allium schoenoprasum*

CORIANDER   *Coriandrum sativum*

LAVENDER   *Lavandula*

LEMON BALM   *Melissa officinalis*

OREGANO   *Origanum vulgare*

PARSLEY   *Petroselinum*

PEPPERMINT   *Mentha x piperita*

ROSEMARY   *Rosmarinus officinalis*

SAGE   *Salvia officinalis*

TARRAGON   *Artemisia dracunculus*

THYME   *Thymus vulgaris*

© SIMON EASTON

Engagement Ring Box
(See page 30)

WILL YOU MARRY ME?

© SIMON EASTON

Texture Print Key Fobs

(See page 35)

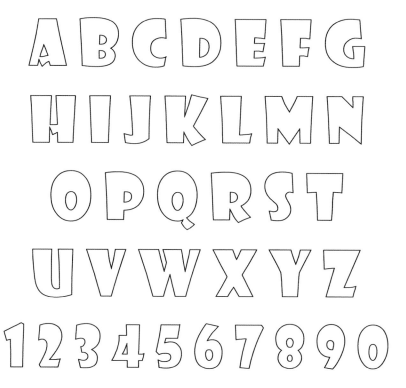

ABCDEFG
HIJKLMN
OPQRST
UVWXYZ
1234567890

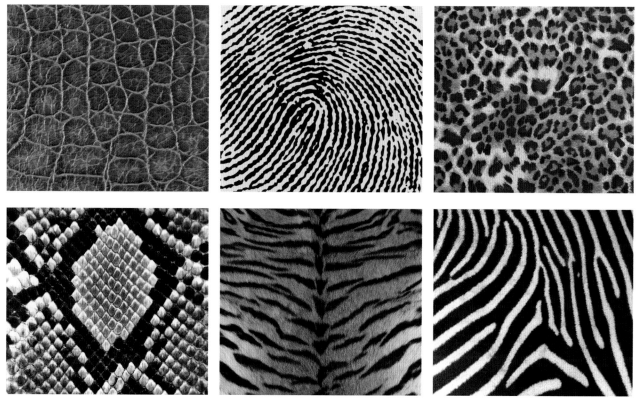

© SIMON EASTON

Mandala-esque Table Set
(See page 41)

© SIMON EASTON

Celtic Knotwork Bangle
(See page 47)

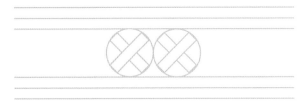

© SIMON EASTON

Art Nouveau Wall Organizer
(See page 52)

LA FAMILLE AVANT TOUT

LA FAMILLE AVANT TOUT

LA FAMILLE AVANT TOUT

LA FAMILLE AVANT TOUT

LA FAMILLE AVANT TOUT

© SIMON EASTON

Dream Catcher Clock
(See page 61)

© SIMON EASTON

Stained Glass Candle Wall Sconce

(See page 67)

© SIMON EASTON

STONE CIRCLE

AVEBURY

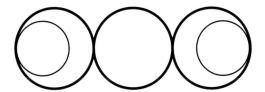 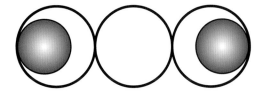

© SIMON EASTON

© ANGELA NORMAN

Mirrored 3D Layer Picture Frame
(See page 74)

© SIMON EASTON

Zodiac Solitaire Game Board
(See page 81)

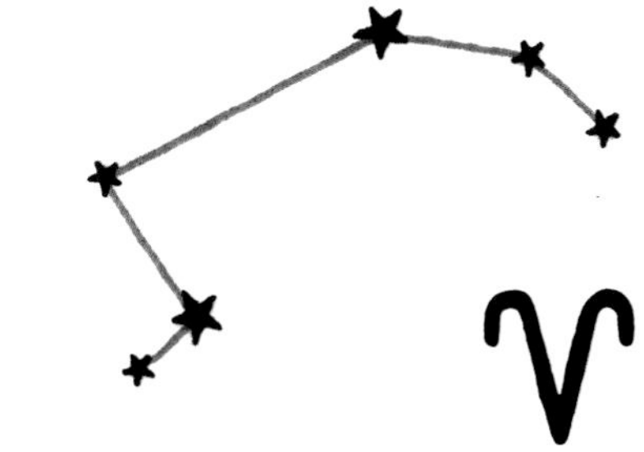

ARIES

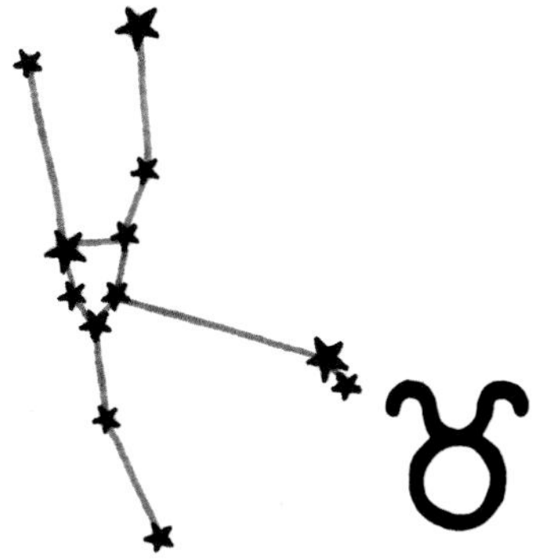

TAURUS

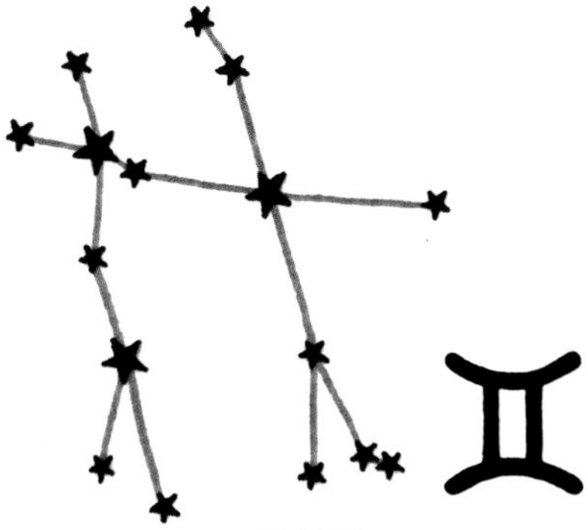

GEMINI

CANCER

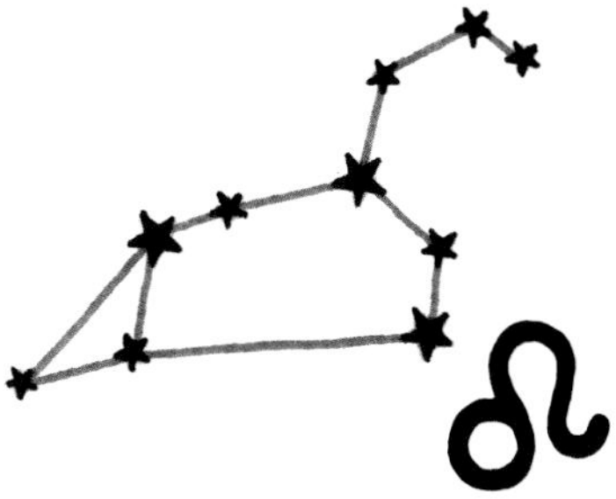

LEO

VIRGO

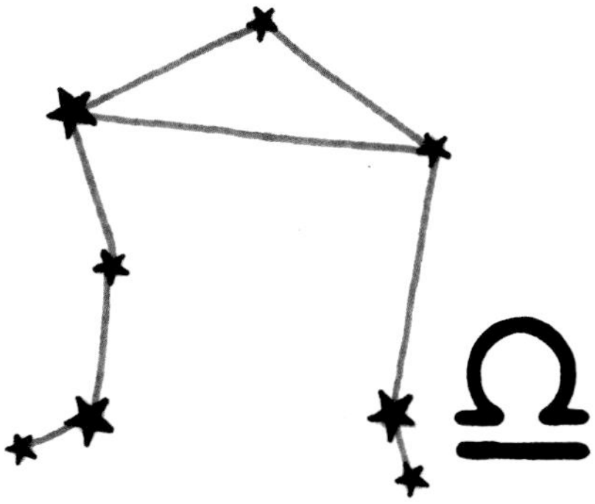

LIBRA

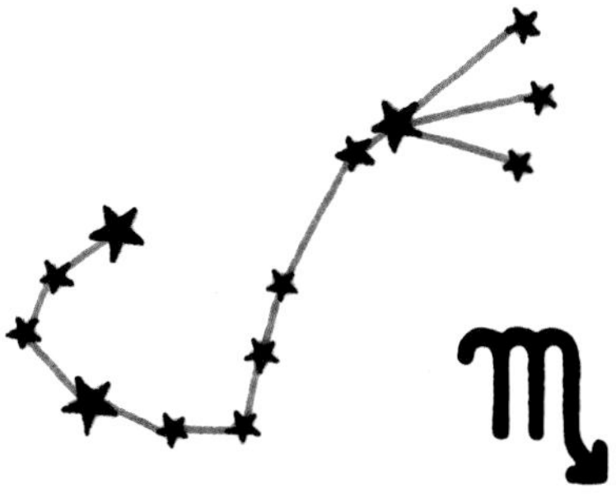

SCORPIO

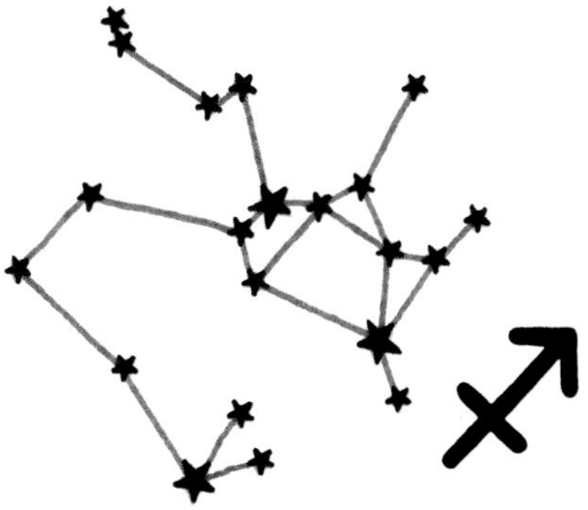

SAGITTARIUS

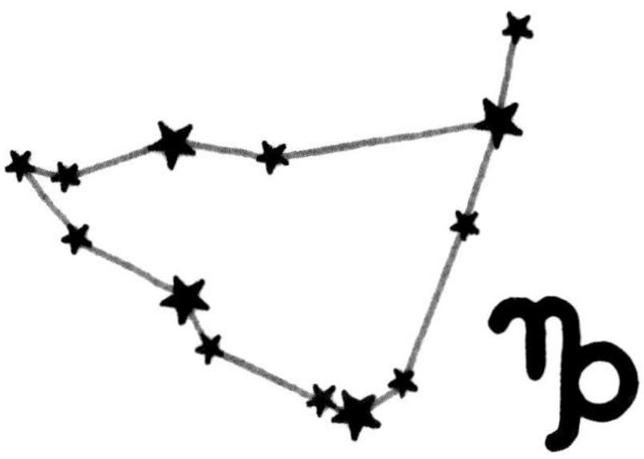

CAPRICORN

AQUARIUS

PISCES

© SIMON EASTON

Dragon Table Catchall Bowl
(See page 88)

© SIMON EASTON

Owl Keepsake Box
(See page 104)

© ANGELA NORMAN

Christmas Eve Platter for Santa
(See page 130)

© SIMON EASTON

Castle Kitchen Container

(See page 95)

© SIMON EASTON

Set List Text Art Frame
(See page 112)

Children's Reward Bank with Tokens
(See page 121)

© The Idol Dead

1234567890
1234567890

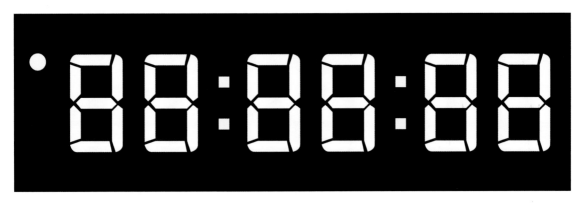

© SIMON EASTON

Reversi Game Board and Counters
(See page 141)

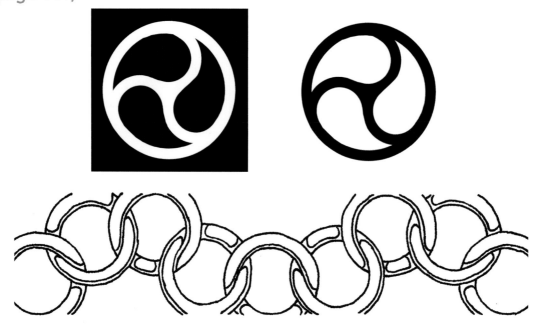

© SIMON EASTON

Halloween 3D Platter
(See page 147)

ACEIKORT

ACEIKORT

ACEIKORT

ACEIKORT

© SIMON EASTON

Resources

Wood Tattoos

www.woodtattoos.com
www.facebook.com/woodtattoos
www.instagram.com/wood_tattoos
https://twitter.com/woodtattoos
Decorative pyrography gifts and designs for all occasions by Simon Easton.

North America

Visit:

www.foxchapelpublishing.com/books/pyrography for even more pyrography resources.

Craft Supplies USA

www.woodturnerscatalog.com
Family-owned and operated supplier of woodworking tools, including pyrography pens, burner controllers, and accessories.

Sawdust Connection

www.sawdustconnection.com
Family-owned supplier of pyrography tools and supplies, including art supplies, gourds, wood, patterns, and more.

Treeline USA

www.treelineusa.com
Utah-based woodworking supplier of pyrography and woodcarving tools and supplies.

Razertip

www.razertip.com
Fine-tipped woodburning tools for bird carving, gourd, and flat work pyrography.

Walnut Hollow

www.walnuthollow.com
Manufacturer and supplier of wood craft supplies, including wood surfaces and pyrography tools, kits, and accessories.

Woodburning Tools by Colwood

http://woodburning.com
USA-based supplier of pyrography tools, kits, and accessories.

Woodcrafter.com

www.woodcrafter.com
Craft supplier of wooden plaques, signs, cutouts, and shapes.

UK

Antex/Antcraft

https://craft.antex.co.uk
Makers of heated craft tools for use with card making, fabric distressing, woodburning, and more.

Bodrighy Wood

www.bodrighywood.co.uk
Professional handcrafted woodturning designs by Pete Moncrieff-Jury.

Chestnut Products

https://chestnutproducts.co.uk
Supplier of wood finishing materials to the hobby and professional woodturner.

Craftsforum

www.craftsforum.co.uk
UK-based crafts community forum.

Craftshapes

www.craftshapes.co.uk
Family-run business supplying wooden craft blanks.

Dalescraft

www.dalescraft.com
Fine quality wooden pyrography and crafts blanks.

Picture It Framing

www.pictureitframing.co.uk
Bespoke framing service, art gallery, and giftware in Berkshire, UK.

Robert Sorby

www.robert-sorby.co.uk
Manufacturer of high-quality woodturning tools and accessories.

Scattering Ashes

https://scattering-ashes.co.uk
Bespoke handcrafted designs to commemorate the lives of a loved one.

Splatt Art

www.splattart.co.uk
Professional frame making services by Lindsey White.

Yandles & Sons Ltd.

www.yandles.co.uk
Woodworking supplier with a sawmill, gallery, hobbies shop, and café in Somerset, UK.

Index

Note: Page numbers in *italics* indicate projects and patterns (in parentheses).